# Over Me

*Memoirs of a Separated Man*

*By*
*Charlie Mangold*

**ISBN:**

Hardcover: 978-1-964712-55-0

# Dedication

I dedicate this book to my family.

# Table of Contents

# Saab Story

I don't like Saabs. They claim to be born from jets, but in this one, something died. In a fire-engine-red Saab, my wife said something that has changed my life forever. She loved me, but she was just no longer sure that she was in love with me.

It was out of nowhere; it was apropos of nothing whatsoever, and it just came out. I was cold-cocked.

I had to respond to her, now, here in this car. But how? I asked her if there was a couple out there still hungry for each other after two children, a superabundance of minutia, and rote sex. If there is, it is not here, in this overpriced foreign sedan, once hailed as a victory of engineering and safety, which perhaps it once was, but appears to me now to be cheap and riddled with trickery. The exoskeleton seems paper-thin. I'm utterly trapped, driving this golden chariot, but not gold, red, and not wood and iron, but plastic and rubber, with my just-a-moment-ago wife sitting next to me in her leather "death" seat, telling me in this piece of shit this piece of news: I'm not her man.

O.K. Keep it on the road, champ. My blood turns to the white part of the fire and, at the same time, freezes as if packed in dry ice like an urgent organ being shuttled feverishly to God knows where my earthly body leaves this world for a second.

Because it sure as shit can't stay here.

I desperately started to search to deny that this was reality, and I started gulping for air, fed through a system of plastic hoses and vents winding their way through the frugal infrastructure. I taste metal in my mouth. What is that? For some reason, I have become a caught fish, flapping on the dock, but it's not a dock. It's a red combustion engine transport machine. Either way, I'm toast.

I would ask you now to allow me to compare myself to a caught fish: it turns out there was a hook buried in the bait. And now I'm out of my element. My bulging, lidless eyes are searching for what will never come again: the illusion of comfort. I always thought the water would be there. Water represents the comfort, the illusion of comfort that comes from a long-term marriage. I thought it might flow in and out of me and honor our pact for as long as we lived. Isn't that in the contract? But it's gone, the water, the promise, and yet right there, I can still smell it. And after a while, as I begin to die for the lack of sustenance that I thought it provided, I start to hate it, its proximity, its cruel taunt… its allure.

Now it mocks me, the water/commitment because it could never have sustained me forever or at all.

I am keeping this red Saab on the road as best I can because the road looks like a cartoon to me; it's heaving and undulating. The tar unhitched from the earth it was poured upon.

I'm trying to ignore a low-pitched, bottomless, inhuman frequency. I start to wonder, as I become the Pollock, the caught, the catch of the day apparently getting thrown back, I have a thought as I am being flung overboard in the throes of death:

Wait.

What if I'm not a fish? Then I'm not really dead.

# Scuds

---

It hits like scuds. Waves of sadness and remorse and loss. But you can't take cover, where? How?

Mortars. Intermittent, maddening, a good enemy strategy. Don't let them sleep. Keep them guessing when the next bomb will come. Terrorism of the heart.

The enemy is not my wife. It's marriage, and it's deadly. The death of a 17-year marriage is a formidable enemy indeed.

Rogue wave.

Hang on; here it comes, hang on.

Despair is so complete that you have to respect it, like a Vietnamese underground tunnel system. I can't fight this and win, and I can only hope to survive. O.K., then, so now I give in to exhaustion. Only to wake up to bombs bursting in the air. They say there are no atheists in a foxhole. I disagree. Why would a God put me in a foxhole in the first place? Growth? I need a medivac to airlift me out of this war zone because of all the growing I'm doing.

Where is Hawkeye?

Put a red cross on my back; I'm shot. Don't salute me. The sniper will see. Wait, there is no sniper, the war is over, and nobody gives a shit who's on whose side anymore. We lost.

# Chickahominy

When you separate, someone has to leave the house. I volunteered. It's move-in day, but more appropriately, move-out day. I took a little house in Chickahominy, which is a town within a town. This means Chickahominy is a town within the town of Greenwich. It is blue-collar white trash, and I like it because no one in the finance industry would come within miles of this place. The house I left is in Old Greenwich, within Greenwich, where all the hedge fund dickheads exist.

I pull into my little driveway in my forty-thousand-dollar Volvo XC90 across the street from an ancient Gulfstream, permanently relegated on what could barely be described as a lawn so that their driveway can accommodate an old pickup, a decommissioned gas company van, and two jet skis on a trailer. I don't think we're in Old Greenwich anymore, Toto. Down the dead-end street, overlooking the train tracks and I-95, is some kind of working quarry. I don't mind this overall, but I feel displaced, dislodged, and dislocated. We call the three Ds in the trade.

I moved in an extra sofa we had, an old desk my grandmother willed to me (it is one ugly motherfucker, but I like it), and a king-size bed, my buddy, gave me (I don't know how much pleasure he had in it and I try not to think about it). There is a kitchen table and some chairs I got from friends, a TV, my son's Sony PlayStation for visits,

4

and the saddest thing of all, my four-year-old daughter's plastic rocking horse, which I gently carried and laid on the basement floor. It is an open basement with a painted floor, and as I stood back, the little horsey's eyes seemed to call to me and say, "What the fuck am I doing here? You're gonna leave me alone in this strange, slightly damp, and cold battleship-gray basement? My springs might rust, I'm all alone, and I'm scared. Did I do something wrong? Come back, I'm sorry, I won't do it again."

And as I climbed up the stairs, I wondered if I imagined that the frightened horsey was talking to me or the other way around. I walked outside and had to stop and listen for a peculiar sound. It was like a week-old doorbell going off intermittently. Turned out to be a homemade wind chime, crafted from some old metal pipes and Bud Light cans.

I guess I'm home.

# Chickawho?

---

Today, I brought my daughter for a visit to the house on View Street in Chickahominy, the Badlands. I was supposed to work today, but our twice-a-week nanny called in sick. My wife, as I had said, works in the music business also, and she is contracting, which means running the orchestra, which means hiring each player, making sure they show up, and calling the breaks and such (very union), for a new Broadway show musical cast album. So I had my daughter today because there was NO SCHOOL again due to TEACHER CONFERENCES, and we went to the other house on the other side of the tracks to lay out a new carpet and hack around. She and my son love this house; it has a beautiful vibe. It has a lawn jockey in the front, but they painted the face white, the victim of political correctness. He must feel like a fraud, not himself, but I keep rubbing him in the hopes I will eventually rub him back to his *self*. We call him Buddy, and with each symbiotic stroke, I feel he gives me luck in return.

The first thing I did upon entering the abode of dissolution was to go down to the basement and bring my daughter's plastic horse up to the little playroom. The same plastic horse I felt so terrible about relegating to the basement days ago. It felt so good to rescue the little fella. These are the little things that make this separation, hardly a word deserving of what is happening to me; these are the things, like

6

rescuing a plastic rocking horse with rusting springs and peeling paint but somehow expressive little plastic painted eyes, these are the things that make me whole because I paid attention to my instincts once in twenty years. I didn't balk at the idea that it would make any difference at all where this inanimate object would reside. But it makes ALL the difference in the world if I believe it does, and I believe it does.

So he is rescued, and my daughter feels this somehow. We have evolved into disbelievers, into a society that truly believes in nothing, holds nothing accountable, nothing above ourselves, nothing above what we make, what we drive, where we eat, and who we lie to, including ourselves. But I think listening and following some kind of inner voice is the path to quote-unquote God. I don't believe in any ridiculous religion whatsoever, but I do believe in something. Because of, and perhaps only because of, the path I had chosen to deny the possibility of finding some sort of connection with the "universe" has been such an abysmal failure for me. This lack of faith has failed for all of us. Our reaction (and mine today as I lunched with Josie at McDonald's) should be one of horror at the waste we are creating, the slaughter of innocent beings. And I love meat, but not at this level. All these little experiences should bring us closer to betterment, not status quoism, not more of this, but much, much less. And marriage is not helping this problem. It feeds the insatiable appetite of the dark lord of establishmentarianism and khakis. We are being Entertainment Tonightified, and we are ignoring everything horrible going on in this magnificent world in favor of conformance.

I was watching a baseball practice for my son's team this afternoon, and I brought a beer. A delicious Corona Light. An interesting phenomenon occurred. The other men, other than the coaches, were dressed in the uniform of moneymaking, not even in different hues of the same theme. Mind you, there is only the light blue oxford, the dark slacks, and the loafers adorned vindictively. It seems to me, with tassels. These men looked at me in a tee shirt and jeans, enjoying a refreshing and utterly satisfying bevy in a bottle, with some combination of horror and disdain. Hadn't I heard you only drink on the Stamford local in the bar car on the way home? You don't bring it home; you come here and get back in line, buddy. You get back in character. This is Old Greenwich, and we don't drink beer at the ballpark. Who are you? What firm are you with? This does not compute. How can YOU be here in a town in which the average cost of a shack is two and a half million dollars?

And then there was the reaction from the wives. Because of the apocalypse of my marriage, I have been obsessively going to the gym. I have also achieved soul-wrecking weight loss, and I look as good as I ever have—better, in fact. But now, there's a mojo going on, and it wasn't there before. I stopped caring what these people think of me. Sweet freedom, thy name is changed.

I was watching my son, but my friend Vinny was watching the women. He pulled me aside and whispered for me to glance over at them occasionally, and I saw it. I am finally a bad boy again. I have come home. I don't belong, and now I don't care.

# The Institution

---

I had my son for a sleepover at the billet de disjuncture last night. We had another perfectly awesome time. We watched Jackass Number Two with Johnny Knoxville and laughed our asses off. At one point, I felt like asking him if he wanted a beer. I really felt like I was hanging out with my friend; what a feeling. I took him home to Moneyville and decided to take him and my daughter for the day. We went to Wendy's, where my neighbor here in Chickahominy works, and we got free Frosty's. It just doesn't get better than that, my friends. Then, an old friend took us all out sailing, and we froze our balls off but had a great time. I didn't think about my wife very much, other than to wonder if she was feeling what it would really be like if I was permanently gone and we started joint custody. Which, of course, is a distinct possibility.

Now I am back here, wondering what has become of my life. My wife must think, for some inexplicable reason—given all the evidence to the contrary—that you are some prize I can't afford. You don't want me? You are so desirable because why? You deserve my obsession because you… what again? I forgot. You are so sexy because—wait—I forgot, why? I'm not desirable because why? I fucking forgot. I want you because—wait—I forgot, why? And you don't want me anymore because why? I fucking forgot.

You know what? Are you kidding me? I don't have someone who

wants me yet, and until then, this will be harder for me than for you. But come the day when someone loves me—not in a complicated way, not in a twenty-years-of-bullshit way, but for what I am—it will be a good day.

I have never in my life let a woman or a man get the better of me, and now, at what seems to me to be the end of my life, I am not going to start.

Mae West once said, "Marriage is a great institution; I'm just not ready for an institution yet." Could it be that, at the inception of marriage, it was a good idea? Two thousand years ago, when marriage was "invented" in the traditional Christian sense, people only lived until they were twenty-five.

Now, we live to be seventy-five, and marriage has to endure many more years than when it was first introduced. Today, my son asked my estranged wife when Daddy was going to be moving back. This is a first. Until now, he has expressed only pleasure at my occupancy at the End of the Line Motel. But now, he's starting to catch on to the reality.

My wife told me about this conversation, one I was not privy to, and sold it to me with a positive twist. "I think you just need to put him to bed more. Otherwise, I think he's fine." She's now buying the crap she's selling. Any good dealer knows you don't do your own product.

The truth is—yes, I know it is—that he's starting to feel the burn. And there's no Clinton-like spin control that can clean this thing up and make it go away. Eventually, this boy will need to be told the truth. What's that, you ask? What is the truth? I'd be happy to tell you.

We'll almost certainly never live together again because Mommy and Daddy are not *in* love with each other anymore. My wife walks around in a happy fog, enjoying the best parts of this separation. Well, I think we're about to hit a serious pothole. She thinks she's driving a

Hummer equipped with stabilizer control, side curtain airbags, and a roll bar. But we're in a broken-down Honda Civic we bought from a drunken preacher in Atlanta, who gave us the marital benediction while stinking profusely of Wild Turkey.

This thing is gonna hit that pothole, and the axle is gonna snap like a thin twig in January beneath a fat redneck's hunting boot. We'll keep driving, but eventually—hopefully—she'll notice the old jalopy is on fire, and we'd better egress my love, or we'll burn inside this vehicle forged from bad workmanship and delusion.

Buy American! Get married! Die! Everything is fine! The kids are fine! This is a period of growth! Yay!

Well, ashes to ashes and dust to dust. A worm has to die before giving its body to become soil. So, how much of this marriage is the dying worm—the cycle of life? How much of this new awareness will be born from death? And what exactly will die to give life?

I fear, my friends, that you won't get something for nothing. I just have to make sure this life cycle isn't going to take my children's confidence as payment for our adult "growth cycle." I seem to be the only one wondering if this gamble with their little souls is worth the price of admission to enlightenment. I'm pretty good at poker, but then again, that's largely due to my ability to bluff.

# Q20

---

I had some idle time in my little dollhouse here in Chick. Self-induced. I forced myself to stop thinking for a little while. I drank a couple of Corona Lights and, while in the bathroom pissing, I found myself eye-level with a device my son had left here. It's called the Q20.

The Q20 is a small red orb that fits in the palm of your hand. Essentially, it's a modern-day equivalent of the Magic 8 Ball. It's electronic, and in theory, it will guess a thought in your head within twenty questions. Guess what? It's right 90% of the time.

It has guessed snot, grass, vomit, a giraffe, cement, the sky, an arm, a hand, a corpse. So, on my "break" from "thinking," I decided to give it a shot and asked it to guess something.

It starts, on its digital display, by asking: *Animal, vegetable, mineral, or other?*

I put *other.*

Is it flat?

I put *no.*

Is it hard?

I put sometimes.

Could it be found in a desk?

No.

Does it use electricity?

I struggled but entered *no.*

Does it shine?

Oh yes, it shines.

Does it come in a box?

Women seem to think so, but I put *no.*

Do you hold it when you use it?

I have to say *no.* But I have.

Is it smaller than a loaf of bread?

Not applicable, so *no.*

Is it manufactured?

Well, you certainly have me there. But I will have to say *no.*

Is it heavier than a pound of butter?

Again, N.A., *no.*

Is it something you bring along?

I must say, *sometimes.*

Do you use it at work?

Use it? *No.*

Is it small?

Absolutely not.

Is it usually visible?

Oh yes.

Would you use it daily?

Would I? You mean, do I? Oddly put, so *no*.

Does it bring joy to people?

Yes, with a capital *Y*.

Then its 20 questions are up, and it takes its guess.

Is it a rainbow?

Sadly, how close you are, my little plastic friend, but *no*.

Then it asks: May I have five more guesses?

Of course, go ahead.

Is it heavy?

Let's not overthink, so *no*.

Does it live outside?

Way off, *no*. It's not going to get it.

Can you find it in a church?

Uh oh, shit, what the fuck? *Yes*.

Do most people use this daily?

Yes, yes they do.

And then the last question stopped me in my tracks.

Can it bend without breaking?

Oh fuck. What the fuck. What the fucking fuck. Of course, it can—it's what it does, it's what makes it *what it is*—that is nothing else. And so I answered *yes*.

And then it asked me, this little plastic thing, it's LED blinking and struggling to complete its task from a lack of battery power:

Is it love?

Yes. Yes. Yes.

It got it. Fucking *love.*

And then a funny thing happened—it broke. It made a weird, high-pitched squealing sound, and I couldn't stop it. I had to put it outside in the pouring rain. Sorry.

It blew up. I'm not making this up. It short-circuited. Most assuredly, it was a silly coincidence, but you know, still.

My little funny plastic red orb. I didn't mean to break you.

But then, love broke me, too.

# Troublesome Truck

I'm a troublesome truck. You've done nothing wrong, Thomas. You're still a very useful engine.

But I was born with a furrowed brow and the need to run you off the tracks.

Maybe, just maybe, you needed all along to be derailed and forced off by the likes of me—off your safe, shiny, go-nowhere rails.

I'll see you at the quarry. I mean no harm.

I have to somehow let you go now. You pull away, I'll push.

I'll look into your beautiful green eyes that once adored me, and I'll stay there, in your eyes, as you steam away.

# The Sadness Calendar

Some days are earmarked for sadness.

It seems to me there is some schedule I'm unaware of, dictating what will be a good day and what will be a terrible one. I think there must be some cosmic calendar. I don't want to see it, though. Would you?

It would include the day the love died, the day you found out you had breast cancer, or the day you realized your parents were closing in on death.

The calendar of the future, if you could glance at it, would have a date on it for when you watched your aging father hobble to a chair and ask for his scotch to be refilled—hour after hour. Unending hours.

There would be a date and time marking when you first realized your mother more closely resembled your grandmother—an aging, decaying relic holding on because there's no alternative. She's confused and tired.

Most disturbing, however, is watching her in servitude to a more immediate victim: her time-ravaged betrothed. My father, the icon, literally fading away before my eyes. Shrinking, drinking, and waiting.

Playing out his hand? Playing the cards he was dealt? No, I think not. He did not choose wisely. He gave up too soon. He waited to see what was around the corner instead of choosing which corner he wanted to turn.

I love him. I love my father. I love my mother.

But I can't repeat them. I can't be like them.

They sit, commiserate, and go over the day's events.

What events?

They drink Cutty Sark—of all things—by the fucking gallon and talk about… I can't imagine what.

I can't be like them—or like the old me, for that matter.

I am a reeling vessel in space, with no connection whatsoever to what or where I'm supposed to be.

I am Major Tom, lost in space.

I'm the chimp stabbing at a short-circuited control panel.

I'm waiting out my air supply in my strapping white-and-orange space suit—running out of O2, running out of answers, running out of the will to live.

Let me go gracefully, though. Not like the elderly. Not like the common folk. Not like a shadow with a bottle of air, a plastic mask on my face, a diaper on my torso, iron wheels with rubber tires, and a colostomy bag like a spoiler in the back.

Let me not be led to the fiscally prudent, brown-tinted macaroni and cheese in the cafeteria of the assisted living halfway house to inevitability.

Save me, Jesus? I wish.

Save me, me.

But how?

How?

# Initial Separation

---

I'm holed up in my studio. I'm a music producer, and I built a post-production suite over my garage.

Normally, at this hour, I would be watching TV. But I don't watch TV anymore.

I used to watch so much, and each night was, in part, about what I would watch that night. I would sit, drink, and watch.

I could never get used to how soon 11 p.m. came because then, nothing was on. Then I was chasing the dragon—anything but going to the marriage bed, that abyss of unrequited emotion.

Eventually, drunk and relatively painless, I had to go to bed, where she lay asleep yet palpably resentful of a man who could not provide for her.

Now, I realize I did not provide for her in ways it never occurred to me to do so—or her for me. Even in sleep, I felt the cold coming off her.

That bed was like a coffin without peace. A prison without ever really being convicted. No official verdict, but the sentence was life nonetheless.

I guess the jury finally walked in now, though. Not guilty, by reason of insanity born of and cultivated by ennui.

She says she wants me to try and find someone else, and she is convinced she is not the love of my life.

I don't know if she's right—how could I? Love of your life? I would settle for the love of my day.

So we are separated.

And we're trying to put on a good face for our two children—the real loves of my life.

Every moment feels alternately like ascension and demise.

But mostly, demise.

# Resurrection?

My wife is a child of an alcoholic. Her mother would drink herself into a coma for months at a time. She was only ten when it started, and it never abated. Her dad couldn't handle it and split—Till death do us part? He eventually drove himself into a ditch and spilled his brains all over the steering wheel, and she, somehow, got a new liver paid for in cash and is now drinking it to death, too.

But ironically, that isn't what's killing my wife's mother; it's the doomed dream of her dead husband no longer loving her. But he stopped loving her long before he was dead. In reality, she was dead long before he stopped loving her.

So my wife has some issues.

I married her to save her. She needed to be healed, and in some way, I did. And then I abandoned her, just like her mother and father. I stopped adoring her, and it was too familiar a death for her to bear. So we died, but now, we know we died, and we're no Jesus Christ, but we might just not be breathing. And if we've already buried the corpses, but they're not really dead, then I wanna exhume us.

I want to kiss her one more time, and I want her forgiveness. And I want her to know that I am not her mother, and I am not her father and that I love her. Such as I am, I love her. And then, when I let myself feel things of that ilk, it hits: Remember, she doesn't love *me*.

# Frogs

This is what I do best: I gravitate to sadness because sadness is very strong, and of all the feelings a person can have, sadness is the best for art. And so if sadness is what I inadvertently choose, then what chance do I have for happiness? I don't think I like it. It's trite, and if you find happiness and try to hold on to it, it will, without a doubt, die like keeping a frog in a series of little plexiglass chambers. I liken the frog and its false habitat to a relationship – eventually outgrowing the chambers but not able to admit it because of the fear of what might await them outside the plastic prison. And so we accept it, and give up, and ultimately live for the sad little frog food that comes to us at the whim of the plastic tube God – or, the creator, whoever that is – whoever it is that has made us so afraid to leave our tubes and chambers, lined with little algae-ridden pebbles and fetid cloudy water.

Our jobs, our yards, and our lives are the only environment we ever knew – our homes, our marriages, our little prisons. And so we wait for frog food. But it can't compare to flies grabbed in midair with free tongues. Do frogs get tired? Tired of trying to escape? Does one ever get tired of hoping things will get better? I'm tired – sleeping, dead tired.

# Victoria's REAL Secret

---

I asked her to crack my back today; I was visiting the kids, and my spine was complaining about being trapped in a reckless host. She cracked me, and then she couldn't get away fast enough. I guess she thinks I'm gonna turn over and ask for a blow job. She said women can't separate sex from love, and to have sex with me again would mean we were back together. How can I continue to want her, knowing she no longer wants me? For the hope that we can get the romance back? Come on, what's done is done, and what's gone is gone. Perhaps it never was.

These little miracles that separated couples hope for must be folly. And it must be worse for married couples—wait, I once was one— and no, it's not worse. It's just the same, except for the denial that sex has become mediocre. Which, when separated, never occurs. So we, the separated, don't have to worry about that anymore. We just have to wonder why we put up with it for so long and, oh yeah, why we ceased to be attractive.

I can't wait to not be able to sleep tonight and vomit stomach acid at five AM so I can be sad enough to see more clearly. Because here's the hardest part of separating: she doesn't want me in her bed. She claims we aren't sexually compatible. She said that what turned her on was putting on high heels and a negligee. But in the last ten years of our marriage, she hasn't even been able to fit into one.

I figured out Victoria's Secret: it's that married women with two children could never look like that. An important fact to keep secret, indeed. God knows what would happen if the secret got out… *"YOU CAN NEVER LOOK LIKE THAT AGAIN."*

I'm going to put out a catalog, Victor's Secret, and it will be full of depressed husbands subverting their innate needs given to them by the creator. They would be sharply dressed, of course, looking longingly in the direction of a past where men used to grab the youngest girl in the tribe by the hair, drag her to his cave, fuck her, and then eat elk.

Sexual compatibility? Men and women can't even agree on what movie they want to see. If men could say what they want to their wives, the results would be catastrophic, although the divorce figures are proving me right already. If the ones who shut up and prioritize the "family" were to say what they really mean… which is, and I have to paraphrase… "God, I wish you looked like someone I don't even know sometimes, but for the sake of our family, which is more important than the truth, I must find a way to be attracted to you and resent you for this more and more with each ticking of the proverbial grandfather clock."

Tickity tockity tickity tock.

# It's The Lease I Can Do

I woke up to sign the lease to rent a house for me to live in. An auspicious day, to say the least. My family will stay in Old Greenwich, which has become the lair of the rich hedge fund robots, the house my father built, and the house I grew up in. Now, or should I say up to now, I was raising my son and daughter in the house my father raised his son and daughter in. Now, I must move to a stranger's house, a couple of exits away on I-95.

For the first time since I can remember, I will be completely alone. I hope I don't kill anybody. I will still see my children almost every day, as my production studio (I am in the music business, such as it has deteriorated into) and my studio is on the same property as my home. I mean *her* home. *Their* home. My father's house. He built it from a kit from Sears, back in the forties, I think, for about fourteen thousand. We "fixed it up" with borrowed money, and it is now worth about two million.

We're in a very nice little area in New England called Old Greenwich, although perhaps it should be called New Whitewich because of the void, the perfect dearth of ethnic diversity. This is a hedge fund paradise. It's where the white and khaki strive and thrive. I have socialized with many of these subjects and have been forced to do so because of my son's school-related events. These are "men" who are shockingly devoid of personality, humor, and light. This is a

25

town, and we've all heard the cliché about epicurean Connecticut towns, but this is a town that wholeheartedly deserves its reputation. This soulless "more is more" mentality has been cultivated into an art form. The tear-downs, the McMansions as they are called, the BMWs, the convertible Lotus, the five hundred dollar loafers WITHOUT SOCKS, the combed side part, the bleach blonde, bleached-toothed, fake-tanned, fake-breasted tennis-playing social-climbing "women," who have no substance whatsoever, but believe that they are the cream of the crop, a crop I would consider rotten, this is the place I leave behind. The only problem is that my children are here, and I feel like I am feeding them to the lions, but the lions are wearing pink polo shirts, with the collar starched and raised, like a flag from a country of lost souls, and they wave the flag, and shout "I hate myself, but money makes me good, my wife is a robot, and I have lost all sense of what really makes a man, and I wear our uniform, which lets the others of my ilk easily identify me, because if I don't fit in, then I am a gypsy, a pariah, a threat to the collective, and I for one, do not have the stomach to be Locutus."

# To Disparage Marriage

———————————————————————————————

**M**y wife and I made friends with a couple, the husband a decent, well-meaning man who perhaps pushes the threshold of parental discipline further than I would like, and his bleach-blonde, slave-to-the-treadmill, social-climbing counterpart. They don't quite fit in, but they are desperate to. So we've been hanging out with them for the last year, and it has been nothing short of uncomfortable. But since we didn't fit in, we had something in common, or so we thought. Since my wife told her "friend" of our separation, she is understandably conflicted as to how to proceed. She has not returned my wife's calls.

And I know why.

Married people see couples that separate become liberated in some way. They grow from the truth, survive, and, most importantly, thrive. The statistics prove me out. A stagnant marriage exists in the womb of denial. And unfortunately, no marriage is immune to stagnation; indeed, it is the nature of the beast. And make no mistake; marriage is a beast that will not stop until it has consumed truth. And so, the ones brave enough to sound the alarm that there is indeed a fire, a fire ignited by contempt bred from familiarity and sustained by fear of change, and those couples who question the feasibility of marriage are pariahs, a threat to the status quo. Most who are married are unhappy within the context of passion, change, growth, and self-renewal, and they all live in fear of admitting this. When two married couples related to each other in the fraud of marital bliss, one of them jumps up off the cocktail couch and shouts, "No, there must be more!" This truth becomes a virus that is feared and reviled, and the couple that chooses the path of denial and mediocrity are terrified that this virus will infect them. Perhaps if a separation paid better and got us a table at L'Escale, my wife would be worthy of support. But our separation and pursuit of personal growth and happiness threaten the robots, and so they make some beeping sounds, turn on their Jimmy Choo heels, and walk longingly towards the promise of more money, more house, a better BlackBerry, the new Audi, and an invitation to a proper country club where they can touch the hand of God, or, in their case, rub not elbows but ankles with the sockless rich.

# My Mom

T alked to my mom tonight. My dad has a debilitating disease that literally one out of a million get. It's called Charcot-Marie-Tooth Syndrome. It has nothing to do with the fish that likes to eat license plates. It is a rare muscle-eating disease that eventually renders you immobile. It attacks the spine, the surrounding muscles, the legs, the whole kit, and the caboodle. And my family has been living with this ever since I could remember. And a braver man I have ever known.

But tonight, I heard my mother's pain. The pain of a woman who sacrificed her whole life for her children and then, finally, herself.

She lives now to comfort my father, thinking never of her happiness because that would be frivolous. After all, isn't life about sacrifice? Is it? I think now that it may be but to a point. I think now that if something is off if one person is dying inside as they sacrifice themselves in the name of doing the right thing, we now enter the realm of two wrongs that don't make a right. My mom is watching her husband self-medicate himself out of himself. He isn't there anymore, and who is thinking of her?

I am.

She is the real victim here, or at least as much as he is. And so this marriage is very, very sad, and not uncommon, and is this what we are

29

all fighting to save? To live a life you don't want to live because it wouldn't do to stand up and say, "No more"?

I don't want my wife to end up my nurse. I don't like this whole thing at all. We are decaying relics, completely in denial of life itself.

We should really be thinking less about the color of leather in our Lexus' and more about our human mortality and how we can, every day, make the right decisions for ourselves and, thus, the right decisions for those around us that we love.

I told my mom that my wife and I were separating to find ourselves and so perhaps each other again, and she said, "I'm jealous." I felt very sad for her and yet very proud that she understood what we were doing perfectly. And I couldn't help but wonder how many other lost souls are out there and how we all got there.

# Cable Guise

G ot my cable installed today at *Casa de Separado*. I'm lying there on my friend's old king-size bed (it has no sheets yet, and my skin cringes as it touches the polyester surface; I thought you would want to know). The cable guy was there for about an hour or so, and as he was leaving, I had a strange instinct to ask him, "Hey, what's the rush? c'mon, stay a while." It hit me how lonely this has the potential to be. When I came home, or I guess I need to change the connotation of "home" now, when I came back to Old Greenwich to pick up my son from school, I got a call from my wife asking how I was doing. I told her it was a bit strange and lonely, and she said she thought she would feel that when she occasionally stayed there. I then informed her she would never know this feeling because she would be a guest there, like in a bed and breakfast, and in fact, she would most probably love getting away from the kids once a week in a little cottage. Who wouldn't? But it's not like that for me; I'm going to be fucking living there. So, I have to wonder where this is really headed. I think they call it the best of both worlds. She gets to have me around when needed or even wanted, but she doesn't have to deal with all the other bullshit in marriage, and I get that too, but she gets to STAY HOME. Throw in the added benefit of no sex, which, as we all know, is easier for women, especially women who don't love you anymore, or should I be more accurate, not *in* love with you.

I remember the day that the bomb was dropped. We were headed home from visiting friends in Sharon, Connecticut, and I sensed something wrong with my passenger. I asked what was wrong, and she said, as she always does, "Nothing." But that day, there was something more. Something right at the surface. So I pushed. And boy, it came up out of the water and kept going like a tactical nuke being launched from a sub. She said she was not happy. And she wanted more. She wanted to feel passion again. Naturally, I asked, "What 17-year marriage has passion?" She said that didn't matter and that it was what she needed.

So I said, "What are you saying?" And then, the words came. "I love you; I'm just not *in* love with you."

Thus began the terrible campaign in the war against commitment.

# Bongo

---

I told my son that I would stay at a "Club House" for a while and that we would have lots of fun there. No problem. But he told a friend of his today at school, and I'm sure it will get around. And we know that one of those kids is going to say, "Oh, your parents are getting a divorce." And we will do damage control the best we can. This town is filled with divorces and second and third marriages; there's just too much money here to stay together. Too much time to want more. But I never thought that, in a million years, even though I wanted it sometimes, I would be one of them. They always seemed lost to me. Disoriented. Confused about what had happened happened to them. And now I walk among them, not legally one of them, but I am one of them. We are vampires walking among the married, ashamed, yet not for being who we are, but for being out of place— like we took a wrong turn and ended up staying in the wrong town for 20 years. All of a sudden, you and they realize you're not one of them; you are an outsider, a stranger, and not to be trusted.

A pariah. An anomaly. Having just come from the Bronx Zoo recently, I can now relate, even more than before, to the apes behind the glass. Living in a created environment, a false one, indeed, it mocks them, "Look, here is a tree… enjoy! Some grass… see? You DO belong here!" And those people staring at you day after day, just pretend they're not there. I'm sure they don't feel sorry for you,

33

Bongo. I'm sure they don't know something you don't know. Why would you think this is not the way it is supposed to be? Look, here's some dirt. See? It's all good, now shut up and act like a fucking cute little monkey. I saw their eyes; they knew it was a joke.

My wife let me get a vasectomy THREE months before telling me she didn't want to fuck me anymore. Don't worry, she said, "everyone says it's not so bad." And I did it so we could have sex more without worrying about getting pregnant. That was the plan, *our* plan. So I cut my balls to try and save our sex life, and she said, "Look, here's a nice house in a nice suburb, see? Now shut up and act like a husband. Oh, and by the way, no more monkeying around for you."

I'm out of the glass, Bongo, but I'm lonely, and I wish you were here.

# Woman Target

---

W omen. I sometimes think they have a propensity for manipulation. Perhaps, and I say perhaps, it's an unconscious thing, but I have become a victim of the greatest manipulation of all time. I remember my girlfriend sat me down one night about TWENTY YEARS AGO at Tuscon's, a bar in Greenwich, and she said, and I quote, "I need for me to move to the next level in our relationship, but this is not an ultimatum." End fucking quote. Not an ultimatum? It's the biggest one of all time. And so, not wanting to lose her, I, with great trepidation, agreed to marry her. I didn't even ask her to marry me, and I asked her to get engaged to me on a snowy ramp in Byram on New Year's Eve, of all things. Actually, it's not far from my newly separated husband's domicile. And she did, in fact, marry me, and now, she says, and I quote, "I'm not sure if I can ever love you again like a man, but what's at stake is so important that we need to find out." What the fuck am I? A fucking idiot? Not only is the writing on the wall, it is the wall. She wants to come with me and the kids to Target to get sheets and pillows and lamps for the separation casa. How sick is this? Making this a family outing is like inviting your friends to witness a suicide. What the fuck is wrong with this woman?

And what is wrong with me that I keep holding on to? This is what I ask you. This is the question: am I being desperate because I was

35

dumped first, or do I really want this to work? Either way, I feel in my heart that it won't. And here is where I get angry: I know in my heart she knows she can never love me again like I need her to, but she, a woman, knows, as a master manipulator, that this thing will go a lot easier if we do it in stages. Be it conscious or unconscious, they do what they do because it is their nature. I am becoming angry at women, and I don't want to be. But will one of you please, for the love of God, prove me wrong? I have never felt so used and so alone as I do right now. And what do I do with this?

I guess I have to shut down. Yes, that's the ticket. What else can I do? I must become humorless around her, for why does she deserve it? I need to beat her at her own game and manipulate HER to my unconscious gain. Which is what? My gain? Just to fuck. So that won't work. So, I need a new unconscious gain. I need a new unconscious gain. But I'm an ape, just released out of the glass; I don't think like this; I'm out of my element. It's insidious. The only thing I can think of is to go get my separation sheets on my own. And deny the illusion, the manipulation, and my collusion in this web of lies. So it's off to Target!

# Target?

From Target, I shuffled over to a recorded recital at my son's
school. My son is nine. Here's the thing: I went to school there.
I performed in that same auditorium when I was nine. Same
stage, same curtain, same smell. It jogs one's sensibilities, to say the
least. I make the best out of a situation where one could be considered
a townie. I remember when we first moved into the O.G. house about
ten years ago, this house I was raised in, which I bought from my Dad,
I was working on a rock record with an up-and-coming rock band. The
lead singer and I got quite close, and we are still now, but we never
made love despite an excruciating sexual tension. During this time of
getting re-acquainted with my old home and my old hometown, I was
never there; I was at the studio well into the night, so I didn't really
feel it. But then my son was born, and in we came into the quaint yet
queer community called Old Greenwich. Being a musician, I was
home days, and I built a studio off the house where I could work when
the work came in. So I was in an unenviable position, as my estranged
wife also works from home and in the music business, to go to drop-
offs and pick-ups at preschool and, of course, the dreaded "concerts."
The fall festival recital, the spring into music celebration, and so on.
At these... pickups and drop-offs, I was forced to interact with these
things, these "women" as it were, these stick-figure, blonde-bobbed
inanities. My first reaction was to want to seduce them, of course, but
then I was struck, as they politely snubbed me (for what kind of a man

is not in an office on Wall Street?), by the feeling of not being good enough, of being unpopular. This, for me, was a new feeling because all through school, I was popular with the freaks 'cause I partied, the jocks because my band played at all the keg parties, and obviously, the band crowd. Women from all these groups saw me as a kind of Jim Morrison, if I may be so bold. An enigma, an artist. And so I had no trouble with popularity or girls. Fast forward in time to 5 years ago, I was standing next to Barbie Doll with feted breath from abstaining from food but yielding to white wine at lunch. And I am unpopular? The truth is, these girls were the cheerleaders; they have always been snotty, and now, with their husbands' money and their clicks in place, they have no need to talk about something of substance! Who of them could be served by a conversation about art? Music? "You're a musician? Oh my, oh my, my my." This just won't do. And so that year, and several years after that, I let myself feel like that guy in high school that the girls turned their backs on because he wasn't even worth worrying about if his dignity was blatantly wounded. This had a damaging effect, by the way, on my sexual identity. Having just come off doing a record with a beautiful young girl who would have, in an instant, jumped into bed with me, I was now faced with feeling like I couldn't have these girls if I was the last guitarist on Earth.

But back to the most important thing: my beloved Target. I went shopping for my sheets, my lamps, my carpets, my drapes, my Windex, my paper towels, my phone, and my soap—but for some reason, I forgot the shampoo. I remembered pillows, but not pillowcases, that had the presence of mind to borrow some Febreze from Vinnie but were completely spaced out on light bulbs. And then I made my bed, and I was happy.

That happiness makes me feel like I'm betraying my wife. But this is her doing—no, it's our doing—but this whole thing feels like freedom mixed with regret. Shaken, not stirred. Yet it feels good to drink it.

I can't help but feel guilty that I like it here, at 5 View Street, because I feel free again. At the hand of my wounded wife—the last person you'd ever suspect as the hero—is the reason I've come alive again. And I'm worried that she will be the victim of her own gallantry, that her finest hour will be her undoing.

There are moments when I imagine her being alone and unhappy, and that makes me very sad. But there are just as many moments when I see her making love to some rich fifty-year-old divorcé, him devouring her because, to him, she is young, and she is very good in bed.

And, of course, the newness, the elixir of the sexually satisfied. And so my happiness cannot be real, because it is actually paralleling a new sexual experience. Of course, this feels great, I don't have to live with someone who sees me as a liability. But how long will this last? How long will freedom span into reality?

# What's The Point?

I had my kids here today at the *Villa de Disseverance*. We had a very, very good time. My son is just thrilled with the idea that I have a place for us to just be us without the commandant issuing orders. We had lunch from Garden Catering, a little fried food joint right around the corner. They have a pineapple as a logo, but trust me, they don't serve it. We then went to the little beach in Byram, a beach for the less fortunate. Old Greenwich has a beach down through town. It's been open only to residents of Greenwich since 1940. Tod's Point became infamous when a lawsuit garnered national attention due to a class warfare scandal involving Brendan Leydon, attorney at law, who sued the town on behalf of the downtrodden and beachless. He won, and it was opened to the public. The town hadn't received any money other than from residents since it had bought it from J. Kennedy Todd in 1925. Actually, when Tod died in 1925, he gave the 147 waterfront acres to the Columbia-Presbyterian Hospital, which was used as a nurses' retreat. Finally, in 1940, the town bought this most pristine sanctuary from the Hospital for $550,000. As I said, Greenwich has never asked for any money from the government since then for hurricane and flood relief and whatnot, an anomaly for a town in any state, but that didn't stop the liberal rhetoric, and the fear and accusation of racism won as it tends to, and it was opened to the public. Of course, this is Greenwich, and they just made it rather expensive and mildly difficult to get in. But back to Byram. The "other beach" on the other side of town, near here, Chickahominy, in the undesirable underbelly of Greenwich. But when my kids and I got there, a funny thing happened: it was deserted. I very much doubt the Old Greenwich beach had anything less than a thousand moms and nannies and little Tylers and Tiffanys. But most people in Chickahominy work, so there isn't as much leisure time here in blue-collar land. As a matter of fact, it's quieter here than in Old Greenwich because people who live here are blowing the leaves of the rich. Old Greenwich is the nicest little trailer park in the Universe. 1/64th of an acre with a saltbox on it is worth two million. But in the summer, it is LOUD. The second-class citizen lawn crews wreak havoc on the peace and tranquility the Hedgies thought they were buying into. But here in Byram and Chickahominy (virtually sister towns), it is quiet as an urban church mouse. So we played at the playground with the background of Long Island Sound, and we threw the ball, and we ran around in the sand, and it was magical. There was no sonic backdrop of rich white women loudly proclaiming their manicure dilemmas.

There was a noticeable lack of Hedge fund dialogue. An aside: I was at the gym yesterday, and two Hedgies were in separate stalls in the shower, loudly promulgating that you could still find a decent townhouse in Greenwich for one-fifth. Maybe one-sixth. The timbre of these voices echoing in the gym bathroom was cocky and yet pathetic. They must suck their thumbs in a dark corner of the trading room floor. Back to the beach: We came home, here; View Street and their mother showed up for dinner. She darkened the mood significantly, but that is understandable. So we ordered food from a great Italian Deli right across Hamilton Ave, even closer to me than Garden Catering, and got a pizza and some salad. My wife's mood continued to be dark, and I asked her to quit it. She did her best, but our relationship is so damaged and so elongated that it is hard to see this thing as a means to get back together. But here is the part that kills me: when it was time for them to go, my daughter broke down. She is four. She had never cried to stay with Daddy before, and she wouldn't stop. My insides wanted out. My heart broke completely, and I felt like dying. And this is what we do in the name of passion for ourselves. Of course, she'll survive, but did we just imprint a terrible memory into her that perhaps we will repeat again and again? Will this, in some way, define her, and is that acceptable? The truth is, I'm here, and there is no going back. And what will be will be. But when my daughter asks for a Daddy snuggle tonight, she won't get one.

# Fire and Nail Polish

---

I took this place in great part because it has a fireplace. So it is early May, the first, in fact, and it is still cold and rainy, God damned global warming. Anyhow, I light the fire every night, and it not only takes the chill and dampness out of the air but gives me something much more. Movement. Life. Burning. Something is not stagnating. Indeed, something in constant motion, its nature is to change, to grow, to burn, to feed.

Since I was a kid spending weekends in my Grandparents' house in Vermont, not far from Mount Snow, I would spend hours watching the fire. The flames never repeat themselves, constantly licking and reaching upwards. Never a pattern. Fire is life itself, as it should be.

Like the ocean, in constant motion, tides in and out and in and out and up and down and water where it shouldn't be and where it's not supposed to be and moving always, to please itself. Not governed by anything. I could watch the water forever. I have always been drawn to fire and water, but for the last ten or so odd years, I can't remember the last time I took it upon myself to go to the beach, which is two minutes away (except on the weekends, when Old Greenwich becomes the fucking Hamptons). I can't remember in recent history when I prioritized what I have always known as a return to peace and harmony. Why? What happened?

I took the kids to the beach on the weekends, feeling like I was not a member of this club but a visitor on someone else's account. But I GREW UP THERE. I smoked hash every day on that beach, and I should feel like it's mine. It is mine. It is not theirs, those yuppy scum clogging the tiny concession stand with their impatient attitude directed with contempt and palpable disapproval verging on hate at the poor high school kids just learning about having a job, something these rich fucks don't instill in their BMW spawn.

And here on this beach, once my sacred land, because it sits on the sea, and because it raised me, as I traversed its trails in my acid-induced un-reality/reality, grasping for life on a deadwood walking stick, thinking of everything, feeling everything, but mostly absorbing the essence of the earth, the reverence of it, the completeness of it for me as a human visitor to its timeless truth… these beasts of consumer burden made me feel shame here because I didn't make enough money.

I blame myself for letting them get to me. I will never make that mistake again. That's my water, my trails, my lost deer looking for some scrap of undeveloped land, sometimes swimming to their death in hopes of finding it.

I would go with them now, into the water, to certain death, rather than staying on these tainted shores.

Let us swim away, dear deer, away from the talk of Louis Vuitton and pedicures.

# The Strip Club
# as a Societal Tool

W hy am I still masturbating about my wife? This is very difficult because it is my number one fantasy. Sex, I am finding, is huge. It rules. It, in the end, controls us all; it is the boss, the final decision maker, the end all and be all. Oh, how do we deny it and convince ourselves that it is primitive and simple? But guess what? We are simple - as simple as pie. Most men with the financial means start with a young wife, watch her become old, and then, because he can, trade her in for a young wife. Ordinary men, like me, stay with their increasingly estranged wives in quiet desperation because of two things. One: it is what is done; it is what we do. We forgo our passionless certainty that our truths are collateral damage in the bigger picture of socially expected behavior. And two: we simply cannot afford it. But in my case, we can't afford it, but we choose change above security, of which I am proud. But sex is a secret ruler, a quiet king.

Actually, sex is more of a secret agent of our day-to-day reality. We know we're living the biggest lie of our lives: that we have agreed to live out the rest of our lives, not being attracted whatsoever to our spouses. The women watch Hugh Grant movies and take a deep sigh of regret, and the men go to strip clubs. I have been to a strip club -

for the research of these memoirs, only, of course - but how could strip clubs not be a good thing? When it pleases the man, and the woman takes money, there is no pursuit of a relationship that will go sour eventually anyway. The strip club is actually a retail service, and there are many who believe it devalues the woman. But isn't what I/we have done devaluing in its own right? To kill a woman's sexuality by becoming immune to it? We married couples stop seeing our woman as a woman, and they do the same. And it's the strip club that's hurting society?

# Steve and Edie

I don't want to write now, but if I don't, then what is the point of all this?

I went out tonight with a friend. He is divorced and very connected to the single 30 to 40 crowd. We hung out with a relatively attractive Brit who has a friend she would like me to meet next week. She was obviously moved by me tonight because, quite frankly, I am very interesting. I couldn't help but wonder why my wife no longer thinks this.

So, I am apparently out there now, and it feels rather bitter and oddly sweet. This is what I have wanted for so long – to be set free, to be myself, to not be part of a failing comedy duo. I don't want to be Steve and Edie – imagine their life. And that's the best marriage one could hope for.

But I feel so sad that my marriage is actually over. Because it really is. And I have a sleepover with my boy tomorrow here at the Fun Shack, and he is so excited about it. I need to step up; I need to be strong for him, and this, it seems, is the true test of my ridiculous life – to do this thing that is otherworldly and brave for my wife and me but dangerous for our perfect, innocent children.

I took some Ativan, and now I am tired. Please, God, help me. Please, God, give me the strength to get my children through this

47

without hurting them. And what about my wife? Why does she deserve this shit? She doesn't.

But this happened, and it happened. And life is a horrible tragedy, and it isn't profound, and it has no happy ending – it is just tough, and then it gets tougher, and then it ends in a sloppy manner.

And so, what is the answer? To cry, and laugh, and love until you die. That's all I know, and I know that's all to know. That's all there is – there isn't anymore. The Auto Contempt Feature (Comes standard when you buy marriage).

My first night with my boy, staying here in the domicile born of discontentment, was terribly gratifying. No rules, no crap, no nothing, just us. Baseball, PlayStation, Dave Chappelle, and popcorn were the perfect accompaniments to our evening together. A couple of old friends stopped by, and they seemed stunned by the harmony that filled the room. I was, for the first time in so many years, proud of myself. Not a shadow posing as a man living as a slave to a failed idea. I am actually happy here. I can be me. It was a startling revelation.

The only caveat is that when I picked up my son at the Old Greenwich dream house, my ex-wife was put together. Her hair was done, and she was wearing new clothes, with a new body to boot. Everything I would have killed for all during our marriage. And now she is taking pride in her appearance? It's like a nightmare, or more accurately, a Rod Serling script. It's the oldest cliché in the book: Now you choose to look good?

Here's the question: did she dress up for me? She knew I was coming, so it's possible. But does that even matter? I went up to her and, without thinking, kissed her on the lips and held her, and she held me back. I saw a woman, not an old partner, who inspires contempt when you walk into the office. Marriage has an auto-contempt feature; it kicks in without fail after a certain point. So, something is good already, something that has come out of this situation. Actually, everything is good so far.

And then there is the sadness, the child conceived by the canard of societal mores. We are failures, right? I don't feel like one right now, but it's there, under the surface, always. Or, more to the point, the worry that we will fuck up our kids because separation/divorce will always have that effect. And then I think of all the marriages that follow these rules and suck. Then, I think of all the children of marriages that have lasted, and they are absolutely no better off than anyone else from a different perspective.

I am from a great marriage that lasts still, and both my sister and I are headed inevitably towards living alone, or, as you people call it, divorce. Divorced from what? Mediocrity? Divorced from playing a role in which I do not fit? Yes. Divorce. I divorce myself from this charade. I renounce it. I condemn it. I call for an inquiry into the legitimacy of it. I call a hearing. I think we need a committee formed to question its value to society.

# The Ring (and gloves) Are Comin' Off.

I noticed today that her ring has come off. I know in my heart it will never go back on again.

I told her it was a bit of a surprise, considering I thought one took off their ring after the divorce. True, I took mine off seven months ago, but that was on the day she told me she was not in love with me anymore; I feel that was a justified response. Her taking off her ring seems to me like a different statement entirely.

Here is my initial reaction to this event: OUCH!

She's all looking hot, and finally, her hair isn't all over the place, and she is all of a sudden not wearing her workout clothes ALL FUCKING DAY LONG. And now she is free and easy, with no ring to feel taken, and isn't she terrific? I know that we shouldn't be together, I guess, but there is something about a woman taking off her ring during a separation. It's like she's walking around with her tits hanging out.

I had my son last night, and I brought him to his ball game this morning. I met the in-laws there. There, among the insiders, the marrieds, the gutless preps. But I must say some of the women were very well put together, finally for me. I don't want them anymore; it would be like cross-species breeding. But there was my old friend, my first wife, and, believe me, my only one, for I will never do this again. And I am reminded of Roy Scheider in Jaws 2 when he tells the committee, "I'm not gonna go through that Hell again."

So there she is, sitting with my precious daughter, and this whole thing starts to feel like shit—like a huge, steaming pile of worthless shit. My poor, beautiful four-year-old baby about to become a victim in some way, shape, or form in this expedition of selfish discovery sits on her little fold-up chair, watching her partner—her beloved brother—playing ball, completely unaware of what we are potentially doing to her.

Nor does he.

I had a vision of the future, and it made me sick.

She's gonna find some rich fifty-five-year-old, perhaps a really well-kept sixty-year-old, and for him, my wife would seem jail bait. She's finally going to have her precious stability. His name will be Roger or something like that. Roger will cater to her every whim and take them to France and Italy, where they will have the time of their life. And she will have her peace. She could never have handled a nut job like me. And I knew it all along, but we had these kids, and they're still young, and I'm really sad for them.

But mostly, I have this interminable jealousy eating at me, killing my heart every day. My wife is great in bed, and someone is really going to be enjoying the mother of my children. Why this is the biggest thing for me is well beyond my comprehension. Because of the male ego? Of course, but it's more evil than that - it's a cancer. It may be my undoing. And when she finally tells me that she has met a man, and his name is Roger, and "I have feelings for him," it may be rather unpleasant, shall we say.

# Tassels

---

There is a couple we hung out with within the last year, prior to the invasion and consequent utter destruction of my heart. He, a money guy, balding, insecure, mean, and she, a flibbertigibbet, blonde, one dimensional, obsessed with herself, but more interestingly, they both are completely consumed with fitting in with the "right crowd" in Old Greenwich.

There are certain someones who make so much fucking money that they are preordained as the leaders of the social order here. I have spent time with these people. I have been told by certain of these men that indeed they philander, and indeed they are laughing all the way to the Greenwich cliché. I have also spent time with some of these women who get drunk in short order and complain to me that they are sick of the same old dick. Literally sick of the same physical penis.

The hair on the back, the bad smell, the arrogance- all part of the package of marriage, apparently- but having the same old darned dangling phallus is the straw that broke the vapid blonde's back. He couldn't care less. How could being sick of being with the same old vagina get him further up on the ladder to opulence? And here lies their link, their connection: money and the possibility of becoming one of the popular ones at Innis Arden Country Club, one of the anointed rich and up-and-comings, a person who needs no introduction to the maître d' becomes the overriding passion for them both—over raising kids, over truth, over love, over themselves and over each other. But get a load of those terrific tassels!

Look Ma! No socks!

# I Want My Wife and a Young Sheryl Crow

This, my someday-to-be ex-wife, is the same woman who embarrassed me in front of my friends because she was so overweight and so shut off, and so not self-aware. But she, in the blink of an eye, has woken up and lost the weight, the harbinger of our undoing, and has become a woman I could love. And, believe it or not, I am starting to love her for perhaps the first time, and as much as I want to have other women, it might not be in my future because I want my wife so very badly for the first time in a seventeen-year-old marriage.

I am completely fucked and sitting squarely inside a horrible conundrum. At times like these, I almost want to pray to some God who could help me. But, of course, that is ridiculous – there is no God, and there is no hope for a timeless cynic like me, a musician, a songwriter, an idiot. I have always been an idiot. Idiotic things have always followed me, watched over me, and seen to it that my life would be consistently peppered with ridiculous situations.

To wit, back at the start of my career, I was Sinead O'Connor's guitar player at Madison Square Garden at the Bob Dylan tribute. I'd arrived, right? No, look up, silly; there's the idiot cloud overhead.

Sinead had just torn up a picture of the Pope on Saturday Night Live two days prior. We walked onstage, and thirty thousand people booed us off. What a way to go.

I remember Chris Kristofferson leaning into Sinead and saying, "Don't let the bastards get you down." I've respected him ever since. I also liked him in Blade, but then there's not a vampire movie I don't like.

The thing I remember most about that day, though, is not being booed off the biggest stage in the world; the thing I remember most is Sheryl Crow. She was the keyboardist in our band, and she was very young and very hot. This was before she hit Tuesday Night Music Club, and she and I were in one of the dozens of artist pre-show chambers talking about this and that. I was married then, but when my wife left to walk around a bit, I was on Sheryl like bacteria on a subway handhold. She was very nice; we talked about the album she was recording—a record that she subsequently scrubbed because her producer had fallen in love with her. Surprise! —and that she was not happy with it, and so on and so forth. I did not mention to her that I really, really wanted her then and there and that she should not hold back from her intense desire for me because she saw that I was married. I simply talked to her and felt the old tingling, gut-soaking desire that we men walk around with at all times. It's like pouring cement into your stomach, and your heart sinks in the realization that you can never have it, and this terrific physical sensation is then combined with an unspeakable horniness. Oh yeah, it's great to be a man. You women just have to show up, and we're all good to go.

And so now, however, I see Sheryl in magazines celebrating over forty women who are still fabulous. But you know what? She doesn't look anywhere near as fabulous as she did when she was young. Night and day. Tuesday Night And Day Music Club. And I think, what if we had ended up together? (I know, I know—who am I to think I ever could have? I'm just saying). Would I be sick of her right about now? Obviously, she would have dumped my sorry ass years prior, but you know, to my point, it occurs to me that you women have it all when you're young, and you throw it in our faces. You rebuff with impunity. But then time happens to you, and you lose your feminine mojo, and you lose your power over men.

I take no pleasure in this, as I am sure none of my brethren do, but now, when I see a young, beautiful woman, I can't help but think to myself that I should go up to her and tell her, "Enjoy it while you can."

I suppose what I'm saying could be misconstrued as bitter. My apologies.

# Toilets and the Main Power Core

My wife is in Nashville, working with a legendary producer. I guess I'm not allowed to say who he is, but on a famous artist's record, I guess I'm not allowed to say who she is. I have worked with the legend countless times, and the stories this man could tell about all of your favorite artists would change the way you think of rock stars forever.

For now, though, I am in the Old Greenwich house with the kids, and it's a bit spooky. But it's not the end of the world. What sucks is that I have not been living here at all, and I arrive and immediately start cleaning filthy toilets. I can't help it; I like things clean. My wife, not so much. The *Villa le' Dissolution* is always immaculate, which is one of the things I like about it. So, besides that aspect, which reminds me of one of the reasons I was not happy here because it always seemed like a "fuck you, clean my shit bowl" statement, but besides that, we are having a good time. I always have a great time with my kids, although they are waking up at six-fucking-fifteen. Not so great for vampires. Or perhaps night owl would be a better term.

But what I am "processing," as the greedy psycho-babble elite would say, is that I realize I have to come to terms with the fact that next on the agenda will be her sitting me down to tell me she wants to date, just to "see what it feels like." It's next, you know it, and I know it, and I don't wanna be surprised, despite the fact that she swears she's not there yet. YET.

And here in Nashville, she can do anybody she wants, but that isn't the place for it, I suppose – all those God-fearing, hypocritical, lily-white, cowboy-hat-donning idiots. She might as well be in Old Greenwich, for Christ's sake. Just replace the cowboy hat with a balding head and a polo shirt. But there will come a time and a place where she will finally admit to herself, and then to me, that she wants to experience dating and then sex. So I have to tell Scotty to borrow power from the main power core, stretch the Dilithium crystals to their limit, and give me all she's got on the shields.

I have to be ready for that attack because right now, the thought of some other guy making love to her puts me on the edge of reason. It makes me sick – physically sick. Imagine someday down the road, me telling her because at that point we will be "just friends"; imagine me telling her that I want the truth….. Was he better than me? And, of course, let's all say it together: "IT WAS JUST DIFFERENT".

And I would push some more and ask, "Was it great?" and she would say slowly, painfully – not wanting to lie to me anymore – she would look up at me with her "I don't want to hurt you anymore" eyes... and she will say, "yes."

I have to put myself in that conversation and not feel like vomiting. I have to prepare myself for that, and I have to start now because I need a lot of prep time to get ready for that scene. Because when the big director in the sky shouts "ACTION," I don't want to puke all over the leading lady.

# Listen

M y wife called from Nashville to tell me she was on the first plane to Fort Lauderdale because her mother is in ICU dying. This is the same mother that has been an alcoholic for her whole life. This is the same woman that used to wake her when she was ten years old at three in the morning shouting "WHERE IS MY FUCKING VODKA? I KNOW YOU HID MY VODKA!!" This is the same woman whose husband left her because she became a disgusting drunk and ceased taking care of her two kids and jumped head first into plastic gallon bottles of Georgi vodka. Why did she jump into these bottles? Her three year old son died while she was away on vacation of some bizarre disease related to slight retardation and heart problems. She never got to say goodbye. This is a woman I have made fun of as long as I have known her because she is a freak, and she was a derelict mother to my wife. She used to get drunk and forget to pick her daughter up from Brownies meetings, and this ten year old girl would wait for hours. This is a woman who flipped a car over, drunk, on the way to see her daughter in some play. And that was a good day, because at least she attempted to get to the play. This is a woman that paid cash for a new liver because insurance wouldn't cover it due to her alcoholic past. This is a woman whose husband left her and her kids behind but pretended to be a responsible parent only to add mellifluously to the abject dysfunction of his children. And she lay dying now, alone not even breathing on her own. She is probably dying because she just recently contacted an old friend, a suitor, she called him, and they had made plans to meet in six months here in New York. She decided, being almost obese for my wife's entire existence, to all of a sudden lose sixty pounds. So she stopped eating. She was convinced that if she could fit into her favorite high school gown, which she has kept for this very occasion, it would be a magic night for which she has been waiting all her life.

And now she is dying because she wanted so badly to look good for this eighty year old flame. She will never get her date, she will never feel the passion her husband never felt for her, and her desire may kill her. This is the saddest woman I have ever known, or ever hope to know, and my wife is going to watch her die. What emotions will she relent to?

Pity? Hate? But most probably not love, because of what her mother did to her. But it *is* her mother, after all, and this is shaping up to be quite a month. Her brother, the one my wife's mom had after the death of her first son in perhaps a rather desperate attempt to make up for the loss, is close to four hundred pounds. Totally fried from absolute dysfunction at the highest possible level, he was three when my wife was ten, and never knew a mother, but he too is on the way to Florida to witness the demise of a terrible enigma. To say goodbye to that which cursed him but gave him life none the less. His mother. My heart goes out to them both, I have been witness to this terrible locus for twenty years, and it has been an ugly taste in my mouth since the start. I welcome the end of this unholy tribulation, but mourn for this soul sick woman's tragic life. I don't know what effect this will have on this little girl that has some how become forty six, I fear it and welcome it, because she needs to put this excruciatingly long chapter behind her. She needs to bury her terrible past with her mom, the author of her own pain, the puppet master of a sick, dark tragedy. Now I must reiterate her mom is not dead, and may recover, but I don't know if that would be the best thing for anyone. If she dies, I will feel bereft. She only loved and supported me, she never fucked my life up,

I saw her only as tragic being, victim of this ridiculous and seemingly random series of events called life.

And if she dies, I will feel guilt for all the jokes I made about her. Because she is a joke, we're all a joke, but now she's a *sick* joke. And now, all of a sudden, it's not so funny. I would like to have said goodbye, but I don't think I will ever get to say it. I'll never get to say I'm sorry about your first son, I'm sorry your husband never loved you, and I'm sorry for all the snide jokes I made about how fucked up you are. I'm fucked up too, but you always knew that, and on some level that was our bond. Though your eccentricities sometimes horrified me they also amused me, and made me feel closer to you. I hope you can hear me somehow; I don't want you to die alone. I will miss the way you always started every sentence with "Listen", as though I wouldn't otherwise. (Although you may have been right). I will miss making you laugh, which I always seemed to do, and you ain't an easy audience believe me. I will miss the way you painstakingly researched holistic remedies for one of my countless ailments, and clipped articles and called to tell me to take more B12 and less Zinc and blah blah blah. I will miss the uncomfortable holiday dinners with our ridiculous family, filled with love against all odds.

Yes, I will miss you, you old vodka drinking pain in the ass, I will miss you very much.

I bet that surprises you, doesn't it?

Listen; I loved you in my way.

# Dying Mothers, Cold Wives, and Klingons

And so my wife has arrived in Florida; she took a cab right to the hospital, and walked straight into Hell. Her mother is hooked up to many machines, she isn't even breathing on her own, and I am there for my wife, or would like to be, and here is the weirdest thing: she is cold to me even now. Even as her mother lay dying she is afraid to give herself to me. I am dealing with something dead, but not her mother, her, she is dead, and I am horrified to look into the eyes and heart of a dead woman. Holy shit, what is this thing that she is? I am in shock because her mother is dying, and I am the only one of us that feels our connection.

My God, who is this and what am I trying to prove? Her mother is now slightly better, I guess; I mean there is now no imminent death. But still on a respirator, she can't talk and is making feeble attempts to communicate with her mung stained fingers. Her flesh, as it were, bags of it, hanging from limbs that just six months ago held fat, but now, because of her "weight loss program", is just old loose flesh. Older than the hills. Feted. Diseased.

Rotten. A loose interpretation of her heart. And my wife is the crab apple that has not fallen too far from the tree. Let's examine the similarities shall we? They both want passion with a man so badly they would do almost anything, for example, kick your husband out of his house on the one hand, starve yourself quite literally to death for a date on the other. Let's continue:

They are both rather cold. Something I have come to realize about my lovely ex roommate is that she does not like to snuggle, does not really like to hug, what is it that she does like to do? I would not be the one to ask. Her mother is quite standoffish, like her daughter, her mother is never wrong, also true of my wife. Her mother has been overweight her entire marriage until now, wife, same, and both of their husbands died driving into a ditch to get away from them. Well, I haven't officially done it yet, but I understand the man. And now here she is sitting with her dying mother, or is she?

The woman has a tendency not to die, but she is certainly sick, and my wife is going through this, and all I wanted to do was have some sort of connection with her, but she's all business. But that's how she copes I guess, she doesn't wallow. I wallow. I feel everything, too fucking much I can tell you that right now. I read into everything, and you know what? Most of the time what I read is true. But something you mortals will never understand is that my Diana Troy-like abilities have probably cost me my piece of the American Dream. But then, what kind of a dream is that? Can an empath and a pragmatic co-exist? It didn't work for Warf, and he was a Klingon.

# Nail Her Ass

I was picking up my daughter from Kindergarten orientation (of all fucking things), and I was once again immersed in the magma of Greenwich moms. I am fascinated by what they will wear. And the God-Damned nails. What is the fascination with you women and your nails? After picking up my daughter, we then had to go to my son's school to pick him up. From there, for no reason at all, my daughter said she wanted to get a manicure right away. She is four. I have no idea what inspired her, but I have nothing fucking else to do because this week, it was right there in town. In fact, in this stupid town, there are three nail spas, two hair salons, two karate schools, two high-end frame shops, three banks to hold all the hedge fund bonuses and exactly NO restaurants where you can get a burger that isn't named after something beachy, that costs under twenty dollars.

So, we walked into Cozy Nails, and my son and I sat on an orange couch while my daughter got her professional manicure. Thank God she doesn't know about pedicures. And I watched and listened to the Greenwich moms as they were attended to like royalty. And the conversations of these women were so benign as to stun me into a disbelieving fog. I can't remember one thing they were talking about, and I was just there ten minutes ago. And these places thrive here in Camelot Northeast.

One of these nail huts right out of town has valet parking, and it is busier on any given day than a high-end restaurant on a Saturday night. Amazing. They can't be doing this for their men! Men don't give a shit about nails! All we want is for your ass not to get big.

So, obviously, if a four-year-old has a craving for this madness, it's in you. A part of you—nay, it *is* you. Yes, you're aging, but take heart, don't freak out! Look at women who have already arrived at that terrible place called *older*.

Dye the gray out of your hair; try to condition it so it, to some degree, approximates the feel of youth. Paint your eyebrows on, and apply rouge to give the illusion there's still blood in your cheeks. Accessorize, perfume, and finally, paint the nails.

You know what? We call that polishing a turd in the trade.

# Creases and RBIs

I have been in our Old Greenwich house for a week with my kids while my wife is tending to her dying mother in Florida.

I walk past their little Merrills and marvel at the little creases and folds and dirt spots that represent the anatomy of their feet. How they walk, and maybe where. But these little shoes hold their feet when I'm not there, and these little foot covers remind me that they go on when I'm not there, and I love them so much that I cry every time I walk by these vehicles of my children's journeys through life.

What shoes will I never see? What creases and folds will I miss? I don't know, but for now, I am tracking them and feeling every move they make, and a lot of the time, I'm part of their journey, and I remember looking down at their feet and thinking, "I was here."

Anyway, my wife arrived home from Florida at about two in the morning. I threw a sleeping bag down by the foot of my son's bed and crashed. I didn't want her to wake me up in "our" bed and have to vacate like a seat filler at the Grammy's.

When she is in Old Greenwich, I go to the little house in Chickahominy. So, as I got up to leave at about two fifteen in the morning, she was standing there, talking about something or other. I didn't hear her words; I just had to all of a sudden get the fuck out of there.

So, at two thirty in the morning, I got into my stupid Volvo SUV and braved the domain of the Old Greenwich police force, for at that hour, you know who was driving home. Of course, in my case, I had been asleep for two hours, but I am confident I would not have passed the sobriety checkpoint.

Luckily, I arrived home and was greeted by my reverse racist lawn jockey, Buddy. I was immediately comforted by my little safe house.

At 9:30 this morning, my phone rang, and, of course, my wife needed me to take my son to his ball game. I have never missed one, but I was going to be a smidge late to this one. I arrived in time to see him hit an RBI, and then we went home.

I walked into the Old Greenwich house, and there she was – unfortunately, looking beautiful. I gave her a hug and, of course, immediately felt that her hug was different from mine. Yes, her mom is sick, and she is tired, but I am sick and tired. I know people who come back from funerals and fuck like mad to feel life. I don't want to hear any shit that this was not a good time for a connection to be made. IT IS NEVER A FUCKING GOOD TIME WITH HER.

So I removed myself from this fallacious embrace, and we talked about some bullshit.

Since I had left ten hours ago, the house looked like shit already. I'll never get used to that.

I walked upstairs to get some of my things, and she came up to talk about the minutiae of her mother's condition, as well as some story about a woman on the plane who got drunk and was calling everybody an asshole. I was sitting on a chair on the other side of the room, and she was on the bed. After an appropriate time of listening to these fascinating stories about her mother's cotton mouth and the depraved condition of her despair, I got up and walked to the bed and lay down next to her.

I held her; it felt amazing to me. I held up her hand and stroked

67

her little fingers. I think one of the things I first fell in love with was her hands – beautiful little hands. And here they were, and I couldn't remember the last time I held them and looked at them the way I used to. But I did, and I rubbed her back, and then I leaned over and kissed her cheek. I then did a rather unintelligent thing; I asked her if she felt anything.

"You mean romantically?" she asked.

"Yes, romantically," I said.

Well, needless to say, I did not get a positive response. So I got up and walked away. She said to my back, "You didn't get what you wanted, and now you're leaving?"

Look who's talking.

# Disney's Frankenstein

It has come to my attention that people stay married for several reasons.

A: The husbands are not around much.

B: Their husbands don't care very much about love. Men look at their wives as the mothers of their children, the keepers of the house, and the architects of their own disappointment. Women create this life based on what they have been told by their mothers, advertisers, romance novels, and wedding planners. Oh, and of course, the romantic comedy—the Holy Grail of the promotional campaign designed to sell the illusion of happily ever after.

Disney and his princess's getting the prince fairy tale is just that—a fairy tale. This fucking guy perhaps didn't invent the concept but certainly perfected it for money. Do you think this didn't fuck up millions of girls? It most certainly did. And continues to do so on a mind-boggling level.

Disney has taught our little girls that they can't and shouldn't even try to be happy until they have successfully landed their fairy tale ending. Get the prince—the guy with the most money and the biggest castle. Wear the pink dress, put on the glass slippers, and live only to be beautiful enough to get his interest because even a King only thinks about fucking. So, then, do the only sensible thing: make him believe you only exist to please him long enough until he marries you. Then, you become queen, and then you can relax and be yourself—essentially Frankenstein's bride, created by Walt Disney, a woman who has dedicated her entire life to "getting the guy."

Then, you can sit back and enjoy the big dress, the turkey leg, the tiresome jester, your golden balustrades, and the beautiful, intoxicating power over the common people. And best of all, now you can finally fuck the hot young slave, the contractor, the trainer, the plumber, and the FedEx guy. Because even if you get caught, guess what? This is the best part; you still get half the castle.

# Transcript of a Happy Housewife

---

This is what I hear them say: "This is my husband, Jim." This is what they mean: You are talking about something that I have spent a lifetime cultivating and refining. I have ownership; I have worked hard to get this, and I own it. This is mine. I put up with what has become rote sex, and I have fucking earned this. So give me a latte because I'm on my way to hot yoga, and I don't want to keep the others of my ilk waiting.

I have an awful lot of nothing to talk about. I have to get to the gym and meet Tammy, so we can go on for forty-five minutes about absolutely nothing. "I can't believe Tyler's schedule — Soccer at noon, and then I have to shoot him over to lacrosse at two thirty and get Tyler and Chloe to ballet by four. Jay wants to take me to the Hamptons next weekend, but I'm too tired." (Translation): But if I want his fucking money, I've got to shut the fuck up and go.

I have to say nothing of what I really believe, which is precious little, by the way, and let him pretend to enjoy fucking me as I lay there pretending not to be bored and unfulfilled. It's gonna be fun; there's a cute little bistro in East Hampton that has the most fabulous pometini. Jay says he wants to go to Boca this spring, but you know, what a hassle. (Translation): Laquwicha doesn't want to leave her five kids, so I'll have to watch Tyler, Richard, and Eva.

Do I have a choice? In theory, if I tell the truth about what I really am, then I lose not only my meal ticket but my pedicure ticket, my Range Rover ticket, my country club ticket, my identity ticket, and my entire reason for being ticketed. How, in God's name, could I afford to highlight my hair? No tennis at ten? No lunch at the Beach House? No, Prada? NO NANNY? ARE YOU INSANE?

Breath — Reboot:

I can't wait to go to the Hamptons next weekend, suck it up, literally, get it over with, and get back to my life. Are we still on for Thursday for girl's night? Did you hear about Dan at the gym? You know, the hot black trainer — well, he's fooling around with Mary Anne. Can you believe it? Doug was living at the Hyatt and hired Prager and Myers; can you believe it? He did the Trumps — one of them, at least. Mary Anne's gonna end up in Westport, mark my words.

Oh my God, I forgot to tell you, Mr. Mackeninni, he teaches third grade — he has no balls whatsoever because he is a teacher, which is not a man. You are not a man unless you work for a hedge fund and get half a million dollars for a bonus. Well, he is leaving Old Greenwich and going to teach in Port Chester, PORT CHESTER!

I know, but you know, men who teach children — well, something is wrong. Men belong on the trading floor, working diligently towards a massive heart attack because of the inconceivable pressure we mindless white debutantes put on them — not just to provide, but to afford an opulent and degenerate lifestyle that serves humanity not at all, not even a little bit. Do you want to get a Misto?

# The Woman Haters Club

I went to a woman hater's party tonight. All the men were divorced or separated. I had a great time trashing women - like women do over coffee about their men. Let's face it, let's admit it: sexism is natural, my friends, and once we realize we can talk about choosing sides of our own kind, we can begin to negotiate with the enemy. Where the bullsh*t ends, the truth begins, and then - and only then - can we find common ground, although, based on tonight, there is no common ground whatsoever between men and women. Men finance a billion-dollar industry catering to porn and fantasy about our unrealized need for sex with strangers in positions and conditions strange to us. We admit it. We give up.

When I first walked into the He-Man Woman Hater's event, my first thought was: Oh God, please tell me I'm not one of these guys. I mean, these guys all looked rather old, except for my host, who is my age and I've known my whole life. There was a tugboat captain, a journeyman (or jack-of-all-trades, as we say in the business), a contractor, a guy who works for a local fishery, and some other gentlemen I don't remember what they did. At first, I got the feeling that it was a gathering of losers and that I might be one of them.

That still might be true, based on what this town calls winners. But these are men, all of whom got caught in the spider's web. We, all of us, bought what they were selling: the relationship version of the

73

pyramid scheme. If you do this, you might get to the next thing, and then we'll be happy. Were we men sold a bill of goods? Did we agree to purchase this product, even though we instinctively knew we didn't really need it? We know this now after so much agony and confusion; it sometimes feels like we found out too late that too much wasted time and energy have been taken from us, albeit wittingly.

We don't know ourselves well enough, us men. We are way too horny all the time to think clearly. Now, I don't refer to the men of Old Greenwich; these men do know what they want: money and their secretaries. But the rest of us, children of blue-collar families, thought we were missing something, and these women of ours knew what it was and how to give it to us. We trusted them, trusted that they could deliver on their promise of happily ever after. They assured us that marriage was something we actually wanted; we just didn't know it yet. More to the point, it was something we needed, again, without our knowledge. They cajoled and assuaged; we relented. It never got better; it got harder. Still, they must know what they're doing, mustn't they? Kids, dogs, bad cocktail parties, absolutely no sex to speak of, shitty jobs, small yards, and even smaller lives.

Now we stand in the back of an interminably long line at customer service, waiting our turn to complain that this thing we bought doesn't work. "No, I don't have the receipt; I bought it so long ago." "No, I don't want another one; I just want my money back."

# The Songwriter; Wrest in Peace

A benchmark today, in my opinion: I ordered a new mattress. I woke up in pain this morning from sleeping on this borrowed King-size monstrosity and realized I very possibly may be spending the next ten years of my life on this mattress. So I ordered a new one. I'm waiting here at the Chateau De I'tsovera. They said between seven and eleven PM, can you imagine? So, I am starting to think about this not being a temporary lifestyle at all.

I went over to the Old Greenwich house to see my kids, and I walked into a pigsty. So I cleaned the whole downstairs, from picking up to vacuuming to mopping. And I realized that used to be my whole life. Cleaning up after everybody else for no reason other than to fuel my resentment for my wife and to remind myself what an idiot I had become because I didn't have enough money to pay someone to do it while I was at the office, being what a man is supposed to be.

I needed a back crack and bravely asked my estranged wife for one. After her half-hearted attempt at chiropractic, I turned over and grabbed her hand to pull her down for a hug. It was like Superman trying to pull a plane from the sky. I had never felt such resistance, and it was so uncomfortable that I was freaked out. But I couldn't go back, so I pulled her to me and just asked how she was doing. She went on about this or that; I don't remember; it's never what I want to hear. So I'm gonna stop doing this shit. I got a new bed coming! Eventually, I have to start thinking of it as the new bed for my new life.

I wanted to give my children a happy home with parents who still danced with each other, but that's not going to happen. I've got to get this through my head. This woman is gone.

Gone forever from me, you know I know it. It was fate, my half-man, half-woman friend said tonight – it was inevitable. We were never going to make it, no matter if I was the perfect man for her or not. She would have come to this crisis in her life no matter what.

That's what they said, and it makes quite a bit of sense. My wife was destined to be unhappy; her mother pre-ordained it, and I was collateral damage. Although she is now seeking to change that, I wholeheartedly applaud her for that. I have got to let myself off the hook; I've got to. And so, tonight – before eleven, because I have left off the last "S" for savings – I will sleep. In this analogy, for the rest of my life.

After I cleaned the house in which I do not live, I brought my son to the bed and breakfast at Chickahominy. We had a goddamned blast. We always do. I am first his father, but we are also the absolute best of friends. We just love to be with each other. It is impossible to be sad when I'm with him, but I manage, oh, I manage. He and my daughter, even in the best of times, are a constant reminder of my failed marriage. Nothing I can do about it; it just is. And it makes me even more upset about what has happened. I hope this will get better; they say it does.* I hate this light in my life to be tainted with remorse.

I didn't sleep too well, even in my new king-size bed; my son scoots around like an epileptic. Plus, I think my new curtains are toxic; they are made out of some sort of burlap, and they burn my lungs, especially because here in the south side of Greenwich, there aren't too many trees, gotta make room for the apartment buildings, you know. And my little house feels like it was zoned for the surface of the sun. So the heat pours in during the day, baking these Target bargains and sending the hot burlap gases over the house. It smells like a horse stable in August where someone has stored their lung-searing gas experiment cans. So it's off to Target.

My son woke up really early and, let me sleep in, and killed a whole lot of people in Grand Theft Auto, and when I woke up, we walked across the street for bacon, egg, and cheese. Then I shot him home and proceeded to work on my Old Greenwich property. I started by mowing the lawn and was struck by Thoreau; "whose woods these are, I think I know," or, in my case, whose grass this is, I have to mow. I now cut the grass I shall rarely walk upon. I think in these terms because I am, by trade, a songwriter. Aren't I creative? I realize I have always thought in terms of the poetic, while my wife does not. Therein must lay a huge cultural gap. Indeed, where one sees this separation as a true experiment with multiple endings, the songwriter only sees it as an ending in itself. In fact, I can see it no other way because to hold out hope is to put off the pain, and I thrive on the pain; who could live with that?

*Weird sexual segue*: I found a huge vibrating dildo in my wife's drawer the other day; I mean, this thing goes in and rotates and has a second arm that vibrates and tickles the pleasure peninsula, and the massive tip moves around, and the base is like a core sampler. It reminded me of the drilling apparatus in Armageddon, starring Bruce Willis. I couldn't shake the feeling that I had been replaced and could never compete with this marvel of sexual technology. And, of course, then it occurred to me that I probably would never again get the chance to try. I bring this up only because my friends thought I was insane, for why would I be threatened by a stupid rubber toy? Ah, but the songwriter sees it differently; he has to.

*I have to* because, to me, everything means something, especially when you don't want it to. Then, it means so much more.

# Sex and The Witty

L ast night, I left Mufflertown, aka Chickahominy, and went over to the Old Greenwich house for a visit. The Old Greenwich house. The house my father built was the one I was brought to in swaddling cloth as an infant. I now feel like an intruder when I arrive—isn't that terrific? My wife and I had frozen margaritas, and we had a very nice time, a perfectly nice time, in fact, if not for the slight chink in the armor that is her Michelangelo's David-like non-desire for me. The perfect work of disconnection, a triumph of the absence of attraction. She is the master. She is the Grasshopper of dispassion.

So then, after our drinks, I came back to the bungalow of termination, Chick, and watched a little TV. And then I had a complete nervous breakdown. I missed my kids so badly that I got in the stupid soccer mom limo and went back to where my children lived—the house I used to live in. It was about one in the morning, and I simply kissed them both on the forehead, something I can't do every night anymore, and as I was leaving, the wife came out of what used to be our boudoir and made one of her sucking sounds signifying shock and surprise. I can hardly blame her; it wasn't like she was expecting a lunatic ex-husband type in her upstairs hallway. But it's still my hallway, and I needed to see them, so I did.

I then dragged myself up over the garage to the bedroom next to my studio and proceeded to not sleep. That was fun. While we were having cocktails, I told my wife it was hard for me to be in "our" house, and she sincerely asked why. Why? I told her to figure it out, and she said she could not. So, I dropped it. If you have to ask the price of sadness during separation, then you can't afford it.

Anyway, I woke up over the garage in time to get to my son's baseball game. I got there, exhausted and depressed, and watched the worst little league team in the history of man, appropriately named the Mets. During this game, my wife and I did not utter hardly a word, which seems to be our new pattern now. What does that mean? Are we headed for the final cliché? "Hi, how are you? What time do I have to have the kids back? O.K., I'll see you then. Bye. Have a nice day."

Ouch.

It's every married couple I see now; I ask myself, "Are they still making love?" The answer is inevitably no, not really. Married people have sex less than single people – did you know that? What, fucking is the be-all and end-all of the universe? Yes. Yes, it is.

Even for women – actually, especially for women, surprisingly. Married women have statistically at least as many affairs as married men. But that isn't the proof in the romantically anemic pudding. What gets me is what they read, watch, and talk about. Basically, just the one thing: "Do you think he would be good in bed?" "Did you read Bridges?" "I just loved Clint Eastwood's character, so elusive, so loving, so good in bed – oh, I would go for that….. Did you see the Hugh Grant movie?"

(Inner monologue) "I only think about why I'm not happy with the man I married, and, more importantly, someday my prince will come – and I know there is no prince, but I will never stop obsessing about it." Let's all sing it together;

Some day, my prince will come

Some day we'll meet again

79

And away to his castle, we'll go

To be happy forever, I know

Some day, when spring is here

We'll find our love anew

And the birds will sing

And wedding bells will ring

Some day, when my dreams come true

And so, why marry? For the fairy tale ending? Haven't we learned by now that it doesn't really pan out? For what, then… Kids? Obviously, kids. We get married to have kids that do the same bullshit we did. Rome fell because they stopped believing in the family model. And we're falling because we stopped believing in the model family.

What's the difference? Are we happy as a society that has chosen the lie of monogamy? From what I have seen, it does not seem that we are looking at a successful prototype for happiness and contentment.

Here in Hedgefundland, the men console themselves with 'mo money. The wives apparently console themselves with 'mo Prada handbags.

In Old Greenwich, we are looking at bonuses exceeding Vermont's gross national product. Fitting, considering Vermont has decided to become a socialist state. (Which, by the way, wishes to secede from the Union, delicious syrup though). But men will continue to have their power, and women lose theirs (vis-à-vis looks) at about forty-five.

Most men of this financial caliber end up leaving their aging trophy wives and trading in for the younger version; this is the way of the hedge fund kings. But even the men who stay with their decaying counterparts have to accept almost no sex, menopause, drooping, lines, veins, and short haircuts, but most of all, bitterness and a hostility born of self-loathing and primordial hate for a creator who would perpetrate such a sick, undeserved, and unnecessary joke on his flock of dedicated vessels of race perpetuation.

It is the ultimate insult – to give life, to give life – and then shrink away unappreciated and suffer the final insult of the divestiture of the very core of why you were chosen as a vessel to begin with. Your miracle has been mocked, and it must really suck. And we men just want to fuck; we are so stupid at our core you have no idea. No wonder why you end up hating us. But you want to know what? We're just playing our part in this sick production, too, and life is apparently not about happy endings, despite what Hugh Grant would have you believe – although, when you look at his real life, he makes my case.

# The Gambler

I had my son for a sleepover at the *billet de disjuncture* last night. We had another perfectly awesome time. We watched *Jackass Number Two* with Johnny Knoxville and laughed our asses off. At one point, I felt like asking him if he wanted a beer. I really felt like I was hanging out with my friend—what a feeling. The next day, I decided to take him and my daughter to Wendy's, where my neighbor here in Chickahominy works, and we got free Frostys. It just doesn't get better than that, my friends. Then, my old friend Vincenzo took us all out sailing, and we froze our balls off but had a great time.

I didn't think about my wife very much, other than to wonder if she was feeling what it would really be like if I were permanently gone and we started joint custody. Which, of course, is a distinct possibility. Now, I am back here in Chickahominy after having dropped my kids off in Moneyville, wondering what has become of my life. My wife must think, for some inexplicable reason, given all the evidence to the contrary, that she is some prize I can't afford.

You don't want me? You are so desirable because why? You deserve my obsession because you… what again? I forgot. You are so sexy because—wait, I forgot, why? I'm not desirable because why? I fucking forgot. I want you because—wait, I forgot, why? And you don't want me anymore because why? **I FUCKING FORGOT**. You know what? Are you kidding me? I don't have someone who wants me yet, and until then, this will be harder for me than you. But come the day when someone loves me, not in a complicated way, not in the twenty years of bullshit way, but for what I am, it will be a good day.

I have never in my life let a woman or a man get the better of me, and now, at what seems to me to be the end of my life, I am not going to start.

Mae West once said, "Marriage is a great institution; I'm just not ready for an institution yet." Could it be that at the inception of marriage, it was a good idea because, two thousand years ago, when marriage was "invented" in the traditional Christian sense, people only lived until they were twenty-five?

Now, we live to seventy-five, and the marriage has to endure many more years than when it was first introduced. Today, my son asked my estranged wife when Daddy was going to be moving back. This is a first. He has, up to this point, expressed only pleasure at my occupancy at the End of the Line Motel. But now he is getting hip to the reality. My wife told me about this conversation I was not privy to, and sold it to me with a positive twist.

"I think you just need to put him to bed more. Otherwise, I think he's fine."

She is now buying the crap she is selling. Any good dealer knows you don't do your own product.

The truth is, and I know it is, that he is starting to feel the burn. And there is no Clinton-like spin control that can clean this thing up and make it go away. Eventually, this man needs to be told the truth. What's that you say? What is the truth? I'd be happy to tell you. We'll almost certainly never live together again because Mommy and Daddy are not IN love with each other anymore. My wife walks around in a happy fog, enjoying the best parts of this separation. Well, I think we're about to hit a serious pothole.

I think she thinks she's driving a Hummer, equipped with

stabilizer control, side curtain airbags, and a roll bar. But we're in a broken-down Honda Civic we bought from a drunken preacher from Atlanta, giving us the marital benediction while stinking profusely of Wild Turkey. This thing is gonna hit this pothole, and the axle is gonna break like a thin twig in January underneath a fat redneck's hunting boot. We'll keep driving, but eventually, I hope she will notice the old jalopy is on fire, and we had better egress, my love, for we will burn inside this vehicle forged from bad workmanship and delusion.

Buy American! Get married! Die! Everything is fine, the kids are fine, this is a period of growth! Yay! Well, ashes to ashes, and dust to dust, a worm needs to die before he gives his body to become soil. So, how much of this marriage is the dying worm, the cycle of life? How much of this new awareness will be born from death? And what exactly will die to give life? That you don't get something for nothing. I just have to make sure that the life cycle isn't going to take my children's confidence to exact payment for our adult "growth cycle."

And I seem to be the only one starting to wonder if this gamble with their little souls is worth the price of the admission to enlightenment. I'm pretty good at poker, but then again, that's largely due to my ability to bluff.

# Black Pumps and Green Men

T he heart of man is dark. We kill, we war, we rape, and we pillage. We clear forests for malls; we consume and waste; we take, and take, and take, and take.

Hitler, Milosevic, Mussolini, Hussein. The Tutsi and the Hutu in Rwanda. American Indians—slaughtered for gain. What gain again?

The British and Irish tribes were infighting—from the Aztecs to the modern tribes of Africa to the modern tribes of Iraq, Iran, China, and beyond. Killing, conquering, and then being killed by your doppelgänger in a different-colored cloth.

We are a race, the human race, that cannot possibly survive, and we honor nothing. I am pontificating about the feasibility of love and marriage when, on nights like this, I have to wonder if I am wasting my time. What is this worth, this examination of the heart of man? The luxury of living in an industrial nation that has become so lavish and unsavory that it cares not for the true question: What the fuck are we doing?

Fuck me; I'm a stupid asshole with too much time on my hands. Yes, it's true. I'm in the middle of watching Mel Gibson's *Apocalypto*, and I'm a bit affected. Jesus Christ. What the fuck happened to me? I got so fucked in all this that sometimes it shocks even me. My wife asked if I could put the kids to bed tonight because she was going out with a friend—no, not a man friend, a girl friend. So, of course, any opportunity to be with those two amazing beings is all right with me. However, I had a breakdown with my daughter. She wrecks me; she doesn't listen, and she's so full of angst it's shocking in a four-year-old, and she is Heaven and Hell.

I wonder where she could have possibly gotten the angst gene from. God help me when puberty hits. She was being impossible, and we yelled at each other at the end of the night. We ended up both crying and then I whispered in her ear that I wanted us to be good to each other. I asked if we could do that, and she said yes. Then, a half hour later, in the middle of some fucking ridiculous duck story, she said, "Daddy, will you remember that we're going to be good to each other tomorrow?" She pierces places in my heart I didn't even know existed. I don't know how I am going to survive any of this.

Now, this is after the main event—my wife coming downstairs in an absolutely (because I know every outfit she's ever owned) spanking brand new, shockingly sexy outfit. Beautiful new white blouse, curve-friendly Capri pants from Urban Outfitters, and brand new black high heels, as if she didn't have enough. But I think everything she is doing now has to be new to shed the pall of her old life. And guess what else fits in that category? Tell them what they've won, Don Pardo. The answer is me. I'm in the old outfit drawer. I'm right next to the old fat pants. She put more makeup on in one night than she has in our last ten years combined.

She looked amazing, and I, for one, am tired of being manipulated, albeit unconsciously, by this display of "I am woman, hear me roar," and also, "watch me dress like a cock magnet." She might as well have said to me as she drove off, "In your face, motherfucker." Oh, but of course, she doesn't mean this to hurt me—oh, forsooth. This is about her feeling good about herself. Oh, yes, I applaud you; you're coming into your own. Fabulous! *Sex and the City* aplomb! You go, girl, and don't worry if you're tearing my heart right the fuck out of my very existence.

Don't think for a minute—because why should you consider anything that doesn't accessorize your fabulousness—about a man who you have made to feel about himself like he is a castrato? Neutered, used, tossed away, sexually impotent, laughably unable to provide the needed passion for this fiery bird of prey, with its new feathers, new scents, new pants, blouses, stiletto heels, and the fresh new adornment of callous indifference to what was her man for twenty motherfucking soul-wrecking years.

And so, I waved goodbye, "Good hunting!" I watched a quick change in her face, but then, nothing, back to nothing, and on to the Beach House for some delicious watermelon martinis.

Hours passed, and it returned in like a lion and out like a lamb. My wife came back from her "girl's night," limping and carrying her "sexy" new black pumps in her hand. "These things are killing me," she said. "I've already got blisters," I told her that, nonetheless, they were quite sexy on her. I got the flat, no-expression robot face. Perhaps there was a hint of pity. Nice touch. She has a new expression, although I'm beginning to realize it might not be new, that says: don't go there, I am not going to fuck you, don't torture yourself fishing for a sign that I want you back inside me, because oh my God, I don't.

So, I got that expression, shoved it down past my ravaged esophagus, down through the bitter, deadly bile my medication so desperately tries to control, down back into my tube-tied balls. God damn you for that one, by the way, agreeing for me to snip my tubes and then kicking my still-black-and-blue ball sack out of the house a scant three months later; that's one for the books, in the void of self-knowledge section of the *All Women Are Their Mothers* library.

So, I went merrily on my way back to my little house in Chickahominy, or as I refer to it during hot days, *the easy-bake oven*, and began to process the events that had transpired that day:

First, the fact that she came down in an all-new outfit, complete with sexy heels, and looking at her made me feel quite desirous—and, of course, empty. She never dressed up like that going out for a drink with me. Also, when I commented on her pumps, she said in her passionless way, "I thought you hated pumps."

Well, I should have said, "What the fuck? Are we starting fresh, or are we living in the past? Hmmmm? How's the growth coming, Scrooge? Wait, I recognize you from the movies. Aren't you the Grinch that stole second chances? Maybe your heart is two sizes too small."

I watched her drive away in her friend's top-of-the-fucking-line Range Rover, and I felt like puking. Of course, all that would have come out would have been asphalt-melting acid. I continued in my time with my amazing children. When she returned, she seemed humbled, I guess from the reality of being around innocuous housewives for three hours. I don't care how many glasses of Pinot you have, and it's still interminable.

The true poetry of the evening, however, was the inability to continue wearing the enigmatic black pumps. The high heels, ladies and gentlemen, are a representation of thinking you want something more, something better—passion, newness, rebirth—and then holding it over your spouse's head, flaunting your newfound self-confidence, and then finally having to take it off, shed the charade, shrug your shoulders, and quietly say to yourself, "Never mind."

What will it be next? A new haircut? A revealing blouse? A new scent, new flip-flops, new nail color, new toe color, clear pants to show off your new laser job? No, it will almost certainly be the most obvious choice, the choice of a person who will not admit mistakes. It will be a brand-new pair of black high-heel pumps. Different designer, of course.

# Columns and Boxes

---

I hate this; I want to sleep but am not able to because I have to write. I spent the evening with my friend talking about this and that. She is quite perceptive, into crystals, karma, life lessons, and everything my wife is not. In truth, I am closer to her in philosophy than I am to my own wife. However, my friend, who has given me all the amazing artwork and created a Feng Shui feel to this new vessel of independence—the *Château de Transubstantiation, View Street*— is, for some reason, the biggest advocate and supporter of my odd and brave new interpretation of marriage. But she hears me talk, and gets me, and hears my fucking stupid love for my wife.

She read something to me, something I'd just, by the title, love to summarily dismiss, but I could not resist quoting, and I did so.

It is from a book called *The Prophet* by Kahlil Gibran. Here goes:

"And what of Marriage, master?"

And he answered by saying:

"You were born together. You shall be forevermore. You shall be together even in the silent memory of God. But let there be spaces in your togetherness, and let the winds of the heavens dance between you. Love one another, but do not make a bond of love: Let it rather be a moving sea between the shores of your souls. Fill each other's cups, but do not drink from one cup. Give one another of your bread, but eat not from the same loaf. Sing and dance together and be joyous, but let each one of you be alone even as the strings of a lute are alone, though they quiver with the same music. Give your hearts, but not into each other's keeping. For only the hand of life can contain your hearts. And stand together yet not too near together: For the pillars of the temple stand apart, and the oak tree and the cypress grow not in each other's shadows."

Holy shit, someone actually understands me. Some dead fuck said it better than I ever could. Marriage is better and more to the point, only viable when you do not become one at all, but rather, the opposite: grow as individuals and never represent yourselves as one. This is the complete opposite of the traditional definition of Christian marriage. Two columns? I get that. I like that. I like this strange dead Arabic man very much. Am I alone? Am I weird enough to want this woman who I still love to love me back? Is she a dead Muslim? Am I? Are we out of time, displaced freaks?

None of us know what we're doing. Men walk around, tortured every three seconds by sexual fantasy and desire for women they can never have. They masturbate to porn, hire prostitutes, fuck their neighbor's wives, and have affairs in the city. Some just hunch over, give their wives their ears to grab onto, and walk wherever they're told to do. We are miserable, and you know it. And women? Are they happy? COME ON, FOLKS. Why is the only program my wife will watch *Sex and the City*? In the spirit of gross generalization, I have to ask why the bulk of the books women read are romance novels or mystery novels with romance scattered all throughout. Women love these things. Books with titles like *Open Heart: A Touching, Bittersweet Look into the World of Love and Surgery.* Actually, that's not bad. Go ahead and use it, Nora.

The simple explanation, and according to Occam's Razor, the simplest explanation is usually the correct one, is that they desperately want that life. They escape into a world that is essentially a soap opera.

Full of drama, love, sex, but most importantly, good-looking men with great jobs who adore them beyond reason. Or, the bad boys, most times hotter than the men running companies, pulling up on their motorcycles and leather jackets, just fresh off a brush with Johnny Law. They rob banks kill people, but still remember to pull a rose out of their biker boots and hand it to the woman he simply cannot live without. "Wait, it's the cops. I'll come back for you!" Cut to the most beautiful young woman's face, ponytail, brunette, tan, young, a cotton sleeveless tee, looking longingly with the eyes of hope for a man, sparkling, bright green eyes, the eyes of timeless love, the eyes of a dream, the eyes of what all we men dream of: the eyes of adoration and sexual worship. And she looks upon him, us, whoever this idiot is, and says, "I'll wait for you forever."

But the truth is, and I don't need to even tell you this, but I will because that's what I do: It's a fantasy, a lie, an absolute non-truth. The soap opera, the romance novel, the woman's Vera Wang wedding, it's a hoax, an illusion, a joke. Pandora's Box is now open for business. How can the life's goal of a human woman be to walk down the aisle of a stone building, claiming to house a God she does not really believe in, and end in bliss? It can't. It doesn't, and it never will.

# I Prefer Corona Light

I grew up in Old Greenwich. Most people lose touch with their childhood friends; I have retained all of my closest ones, all of them. I think it might be my legacy: my friends. It has been said the measure of a man is his friends, and in that way, I am a king. But here in the Northeast Gold Coast Hell, the measure of a man is how much he makes, so I don't rate. But in my world, I rate.

And something odd is happening with several of my precious friends, some of whom are married with children. Their marriages are fucked, like mine. Now, as I stand up and articulate the middle-aged man's plight, they come to my cottage of freedom and sorrow. One by one, they tell their stories, which are, not surprisingly, my story.

They don't have my magical View Street, so they come here and unload. What I'm hearing isn't shocking, per se, but it's sobering. It's worse and worse. Sex has died; their wives overspend and, surprise! come from abusive parents. And, surprise! They're unfulfilled. And, surprise! They're not happy. The marriage is fucked. But, of course, they still "love each other." And, of course, the fucking kids. And and and and and and and and and and…

They come here, my beloved friends from my past and my present and my most certainly volatile future, and they give of themselves as they have never done before because I am safe now. I no longer even have the ability to bullshit them. I'm ahead of them, forging I, for some reason unbeknownst to myself, have become the prophet of the sad truth of why relationships absolutely cannot survive. Not really. Not what we promote in any given church, not in Williams Sonoma, not in Pottery Barn, not in the Bible, and not on TV. Oh my God, how can TV be wrong? I got news for you, it's so fucking wrong it's perverse. The whole thing is perverse. The dream, the ideal of what is beautiful, the illusion of the perfect relationship, is unattainable, cruel, and doomed. But we all want hope, don't we? I still do, like a ridiculous golden retriever immediately following an undeserved beating. I will choose hope over reality over my cynical and logical understanding of life as I know it to be. I still choose the promise of love, what I mock the romance novel minions for, and that makes me one of you, so go ahead, feel better about yourselves, for I must be a misogynist. I can't possibly be right because, if I am, then we're all fucked, and we don't want to all be fucked, even though it seems to me we already are. I must tell you this: I am already.

So, here's to you, Mr. Stay-in-the-marriage-even-though-you-don't-really-love-your-wife-anymore stockbroker money maker! You've had a long day at the office, and you come home to polished floors and clean Marvin's windows. You kiss the kids you hardly have anything to do with, and you climb into bed with a woman who puts up with your miserable ass because it's all she knows and is frozen in fear, and so are you. This Bud's for you!

# Jessica Biel

I'm having trouble swallowing. Two years ago, or was it three? I had what's called an endoscope shoved down my throat. They stuck a tube camera down my throat to see why it hurt for me to swallow. Turns out I had burned my esophagus flap off. What's that you say? What flap? Well, I'll tell you, there is a flap in your throat that keeps the stomach acid from coming up into your esophagus, which is in your throat. I burned through mine, what with all the booze and coke and bad eating and all. I have never chewed my food correctly. I *eschew* incorrectly. Since I was a kid, my mom used to ask me after every single meal, "Did you even taste that?" I don't remember tasting things very much; I was just getting through the meal to get to the next bit of pleasure waiting for me just around the corner. So, for whatever reason, I fucked myself and had to go on medication every day for the rest of my life. Apparently, if you get cancer in the throat, you die. So it seems to have come back, and I have to call the goddamned doctor again, goddammit.

I have great fear when it comes to illness. And when you have children, especially young children, it raises the ante beyond any considerable degree of sanity. I guess it's possible that it will go away, and it may be irritated from the fact that last night, I was wailing uncontrollably for hours. I couldn't stop. It was horrible. I had my head buried in my laundry basket full of clothes to muffle the sounds being emitted by what must have seemed to my neighbors like a wounded moose. This happens about once every other week. I don't know what brings it on. I mean, I did have drinks with my wife and watched the series finale of *The Sopranos*. We sat together, watched it, didn't speak, and then I hugged her and left. I got back to the liberation/horror chamber, and there was a dirty shirt my son had left from the night before on the sleepover. That broke me. I held it up to my nose, and it smelled like his little sweaty body. Next to his shirt in the little playroom was a tiny pair of my daughter's socks. Little pink ones with tiny rubber dots on the bottom for grip. These socks were so worn there was almost no rubber left, but you could still see where they had been. I thought about my little girl, who, that day, I had taken to the beach and watched her play down by the incoming tide with two other little girls. At one point, she came running up to where I was sitting, a good way up the beach, and she came running up to me as fast as she could. I thought there was something wrong, but there wasn't. She breathlessly came up to my face and said, "I need a hug." We hugged, and she ran back down to her little friends. What did I do to deserve that? I'm not even around anymore. All this and more came at me, like when the flu hits you. I went down and stayed down. I am still down, waiting for a bit of good news like I don't have throat cancer, or I have a happy marriage. But what are the odds of either of those things coming true?

And so, I just got back from the ass and throat doctor. My doctor is an Indian. *From India.* There are a lot of Indians who become doctors; I don't know what in God's fading green Earth could compel a person to want to look deep into other people's assholes. Go figure. I went there for her to charge me hundreds of dollars to make an appointment so she could charge me thousands of dollars to look down my aching throat. And I thought, while I'm there, why not the ass? It's a two-for. As I have said to her on many occasions, please use a different pipe for each orifice, or, in any case, do the mouth first.

I have an appointment for the cavity search and rescue this Friday.

I go under for this, which I am fond of, but the horror of the night before is what I am most looking forward to. Starting at 3 p.m. the day before, I have to start drinking a shockingly vile concoction and continue to drink it all night long. Before that, however, I can't eat a Goddamn thing. Clear soup. Nothing red (it interferes with the dye), no nuts five days before, no aspirin, no this, that, or the fucking other. So, at three, on a stomach of broth and nothing red, I start to take this stuff. You are not allowed to leave your house once you start down this path. Within the hour, you run screaming to the toilet, and the whole world, as you know, comes raging out at three hundred pounds per square inch.

Okay, you say, that's done. Ah, contraire, you have just begun. You continue to partake of this jug of hell tonic all night long. Hour after hour, you cannot believe there is a substance man has created to drag on the spitting of nothing from your retching anus. That is the day before; then you go in at the crack of dawn (ass puns just come naturally), and they take a look-see.

And now, to the point: My wife found out about the possible foul play going on in my esophagus, and she is all, "You're not going through this alone," and I'm all, "Yes, I am because I am alone," and she's all like, "We are your family," and I'm all, "I am alone." The truth is, I am alone.

Husbands and wives put up with each other for just this sort of occasion. In sickness and in health, right? Well, she's not there in health anymore, so why should she have to be there for the sickness? In fact, it makes me really uncomfortable for her—who now seems to me a stranger, a strange and alluring woman—to see me frail and vulnerable, all decked out in a hospital gown made of paper, its purpose, according to my conspiracy theorist friend, to keep the patients demure, so they won't rise up. And she would come into post-op in her Capri pants and her *Chanel* sunglasses, lower a cup of ginger ale to my quivering lips, and look upon me as infirm, weak, and not making money.

I told her under no circumstances would she take me back to Sin City: Old Greenwich. I told her I wanted to be driven back to where I belonged: View Street, Chickahominy. She is fighting me on this, but there can be no compromise. Her argument—that I need to be taken care of, and that is what family is for—is not cutting it, no *Cutty Sark*. I told her I need now to take care of myself; if you're not going down on me, then you don't have to wipe my brow.

I have, in the long and recent distant past, suffered from migraines on a regular basis. This ended when I started working out every day— let that be a lesson to y'all. But for a long time, my wife and children had to watch me spend the day in bed every other week or so. How I must have looked to a woman who is surrounded by men who don't get headaches, and in fact, if they do, they still work. They make the fucking money. Money isn't everything, but to a woman, it means more than money itself; it means they are being cared for, attended to, and loved. Their men are at the office for them, and they eat it up. That is sexy. Working. Making money. Not being at home.

I did the exact opposite of that and got the undesired effect.

I apparently ate the marriage too fast and didn't taste that either.

In any case, we'll see what the doctor says about my throat. In the meantime, I will tend to matters of my heart, my dream of keeping this marriage afloat. But that is what this is—make no mistake—only a dream, the impossible dream. I am Don Quixote. Our love is the Windmill, and she didn't even show up to watch the battle.

# Curtains

I have a scheduled colonoscopy tomorrow, and if you've never had this magical procedure done, then you wouldn't know that the night before, you have to clean out your colon. All the way out. They want your colon bereft. They want your colon to be alone. Terribly alone and without its usual posse.

Out, out, brief colon.

They give you a bottle—a very large bottle—of what is called *Half Litely*. That is what it is called. It's about a gallon of the vilest substance known to man. You take a pill at 3 p.m., and then an hour later, and every subsequent hour, you down twelve ounces of this contemptuous solution. They give you two "flavor packets," one orange and one lemon. I went commando. Packetless. Flavorless. I am keeping "it" real.

I just took the first course of the bowel blower and am awaiting its havoc. Tonight is gonna be a magical hell on porcelain. Only clear liquids are allowed for the rest of the night. No food of any kind. Especially no nuts, as the nuts show up on the camera attached to the end of the scope as polyps. Also, nothing with red dye in it, like Jello or nuts dyed red. So, only clear liquids? I say to myself, and I say, "Beer's clear!" So I'm gonna get drunk and puke out my ass. Ah, the single life!

(Cut to the next day because…)

The next morning, I arrived at the hospital, and after they made me sign forms to OK the invasion of my ass and throat, I was brought back to pre-op. I was ushered into a little chamber with a curtain for a wall, with netting on the upper portion to let the air, light, and sense of breathing room in. There are ten or so bays right next to each other, and after the nurse closed the curtain—my "door"—I got into the cotton gown. You slip it on and realize there is no way in Hell any human, most especially the elderly, could tie the fucking back of these things. (It's open in the back, so when you go to the bathroom, holding your IV in one hand, you desperately attempt to use the other to close the gap so the attractive nurses won't see your sad little butt cheeks. They try not to look, but when a man of my stature walks by, and there's a chance they might get a load of this hunk's junk (oh, they may have glanced), I lay down and wait.)

A nurse comes "in," after "knocking" on the "door," and takes my stats. All good so far.

She asked me if I had anything for breakfast, and I told her a Spanish omelet, a tall glass of milk, and a bowl of pine nuts. Oh, and a red Popsicle. She does not react to the hilarity I have just proffered. She puts in an IV, takes my BP, and hangs up a drip of saline and potassium. She "exits" my "room." There is a loud ex-nurse "next door," and she is prattling on about whatever.

"Where's George? Is he still here? I can't believe how different this place is. Can I have a donut? I know I'm not supposed to, but Gracie, you know me—special treatment and all, honor among nurses, right?" GREAT AMOUNTS OF LAUGHTER then ensue, mostly from herself. Jolly, harmless, nice, and verbose. God bless. She probably comforted hundreds of people in her time. I wish her well; I wonder if she got her donut.

Eventually, as all we mounds of heaving flesh are, she is wheeled away to the great operating theater on the other side of the complex.

Then, it is quiet for a while, and another victim is wheeled in as my new neighbor. I can't see anything except the ceiling in the main room through the fishnet atop my curtain, but I can hear absolutely everything. Next to me, I hear a demure young woman, probably 30, and her nebbish husband. One can tell from the voices—remember, I am an audio professional. Do not attempt to judge people from their voices at home. I hear them talking, I hear a soft, quiet kiss, and I hear the husband ask his wife if she needs another blanket. She says yes. He goes to get one.

Next, the nurse comes "in" and asks the requisite questions.

"Allergic to anything?" the nurse asks.

"Oh yeah."

"Yeah? Like what, hon?"

"I'm asthmatic; I can't eat peanuts, no lotions, no aspirin; it makes me sick. Advil makes me cramp. No general anesthesia; I vomit violently. No Malox or Tums, no blood thinners because of my last surgery, and I gave the other nurse the list of prescription medications I absolutely cannot take."

"OK, hon, what was that other procedure?"

"I had a mastectomy."

"Single?"
"No, double, and some of my lymph nodes too."

The husband comes back with the blankets.

"You're having an upper GI?"

"Unfortunately." Some polite laughter.

"Don't worry, hon. It takes five minutes; it's the colonoscopy that takes the time."

They hear a faint groaning from their neighbor.

"What is going on with your throat, dear?" Her husband answers suddenly, "It's really hurting her. She's having trouble eating."

"Yeah," says the wife.

"OK, hon, the doctor will be in a minute, and then they're gonna wheel you to your procedure room. Don't worry about a thing. We'll take good care of you."

"Thanks, Sally," the wife says.

"OK, hon."

The nurse leaves, and I realize I'm crying. This young couple, starting out in life, was hit by a ton of hungry, murderous bricks. Blindsided. The nebbish is now my hero. Standing by his sick wife, most probably soon to be, as they say, riddled with cancer. They, still talking quietly, making little inside jokes, are still IN love—even with all this tragedy, or perhaps because of it? I find myself praying for them, to God knows who, and for some reason, I am not afraid for myself at this point, but more afraid for them.

God, I wish people didn't have to go through all this death. It's inhuman. But as we age, it becomes the essence of being human, and it may be one reason people couple—because imagine if she didn't have her husband. Imagine. Imagine going through all that cancer alone.

Having your breasts removed? Are you kidding me? And people do this every day—breasts, colons, stomachs, throats, legs, arms, livers, kidneys, on and on and on. And out and out and out.

My doctor swishes into my chamber, my Indian ass and throat woman doctor. I like her face; I always have. She pats me on my arm, and she herself wheels me toward my destiny. Nice touch. I am watching the ceiling go by, light by light, panel by panel, listening to the beeps and whistles of a hospital and the constant jolly laughter of the nurses tirelessly keeping up the morale of a place so easily given to fear. I have arrived. A bright little room with monitors and flexible metal tubes, I assume, is for asses and throats.

There appears a nice Jewish gentleman who is my anesthesiologist. He asked me if I had anything to eat, and I gave him my omelet routine. This one laughs and says, "Well, we'll be seeing it soon." Funny, funny. He asks if I have any heart pain or shortness of breath, and I tell him yes, but young Jewish doctors always have that effect on me. I took a chance; the room erupted in a nice bit of laughter. I have done my job, put everyone at ease, convinced them that I am funny and should be kept alive, and then, I quietly give myself to the cocktail. Oh, blessed relief from life itself. I go quickly, painlessly, and willingly.

And my last thought before I go completely under is: this must be what it's like to finally let yourself die. It's not so bad—not that I want to die, but right before you proceed to oblivion, there is a nice little parting gift: peace. No heartache, no guilt, no regrets. No living with all that you have done wrong to those you loved most, those whom you should have treated better, said kinder things to, been more tolerant of and seen the good where so much of the time we see fault. And the most relief for me was, for a moment, to forget that I was discarded.

I actually smiled right before I went down. I looked at my handsome Jewish doctor and said, "Nice job."

I floated into nothingness and remained there for an eternity, it seemed. It was bliss. I was cradled by the clouds and stroked by the cool night sky. I floated through the universe with nary a care. If there is a Heaven, then it's gotta be like this.

And then... BOOM!

Everything is bright white and bustling. Sounds of stainless steel gurneys clacking against IV poles on wheels. Visions of strangers poking and prodding. The smell of linens, coffee, and disinfectant. And the yelling.

They yell at you when you wake up for some reason. They yell and walk away. So now I was back, back to my grueling existence. Oh, happy day. They give you apple juice and fruit and a muffin. Do you have any idea how good this muffin was? My God. And they leave you alone after you have farted. My doctor came and talked to me, but I don't remember what she said—a side effect of the anesthesia.

So I dress and walk to the waiting chairs, slick green vinyl and chrome. My wife has not arrived yet to pick me up; she will not be early, but she will be exactly on time. And she is. But by then, I am dressed and waiting in a chair for half an hour. Not her fault; they finished early with my holes. The score is Ass: 0, Throat: biopsy.

So, no ass cancer at this time, but my throat looks horrible, apparently. My Indian doctor said she wanted to know why. I'll get the results in a week. I think I know why: the howling, the rum, vodka, tequila, and the countless Corona Lights. My doctor didn't say Mylanta; my doctor said, "My God, what the fuck is wrong with you?" Well, I don't know.

So my wife drives me to View Street, as I had requested, and she is very sweet. She lies down next to me when we get home to my bed, cries, and tells me she loves me. But I know she doesn't mean *in love*, so it is unbearably bittersweet. It was a nice feeling, though. At one point, I turned over and kissed her on the mouth, and it was soft and wonderful, but I knew to make it quick and turn back around. I'm no fool. It was the sweetest it's been in years. But it's short-lived. I ask her to go so I can try to sleep, which I do for two hours, and then wake up to my loneliness.

I walk to get my car (the hospital is right down the street from here), and I drive back and do whatever it is I do. My wife and the kids bring me dinner, and I, as usual, am wrecked with love when I see them. My God, they are so beautiful. And, of course, so is my wife. I notice, as she talks to me about whatever she is saying, I keep looking at her face, her breasts, her hair, and I smell her. I see she has

103

whitened her teeth; now they look perfect, where, during the last ten years of our marriage, they were a bit yellow from coffee. She also had her hair highlighted, and the list goes on and on.

And this all happens after we are done. If it didn't rip my heart out every fucking time I see her, it would be funny. But it doesn't feel funny right now. But the brighter side: tonight, I'm gonna eat all the fucking peanuts I want.

# Come and Knock on My Door

Had a knock on the door yesterday morning—it was she. I had sent an email describing my distaste for her inability to communicate. This, apparently, is a malady she has suffered from for quite some time. I find it nothing short of ridiculous that either one of us lived with this for 17 years. As my wife points out, our relationship has largely comprised of me being the personality and her being the supportive wife. Much too supportive. She carried us financially for so long, both of us waiting for the big break, of which there were so many close calls as to boggle the mind. But as Edison said, before he made a light bulb that worked, he made thousands that didn't. So, in the creative industry, only the fittest survive. I'm still here, especially now, since there isn't a huge, life-snuffing cancer in my ass.

So we didn't really talk for a long time, and for some reason, we lived like that. It happens; it happens every day. And in this town, it is the rule, not the exception. But one day, seventeen years later, my wife pulled me aside and quietly whispered in my ear that the Emperor had not, indeed, gotten dressed. And now it is no longer acceptable to talk about nothing. And while we're at it, if the only shit you say to me is about how crappy our marriage was forever, if the only things you remember about us are negative, then what the fuck are we doing here?

So, I sent her something to that effect in an electronic correspondence.

The next morning, the knock on the door came quite early, and I shuffled to answer it in my Fruit of the Looms. She was standing there, crying, apologizing for not opening up and for focusing only on the negative. It was a nice effort, though she's not exactly known for putting in effort when it comes to our relationship. What struck me, though, was that she was in my bed, and I didn't care. For some reason, this time, it didn't kill me like it had before. I don't know why it didn't, and frankly, I don't want to know. It was just a nice break from the unrequited lust.

We talked for a while. I took her out for a cappuccino across the street at Bella Cucina, and then we went together to my son's graduation ceremony. He's fucking 9. I mean, any reason not to teach and to celebrate something, right? They celebrated it with the obligatory, rousing rendition of "Pomp and Circumstance," which sounded more like bombs and circus bands than a solemn graduation march. But at the end of the day—or in this case, at the beginning of the day—because God forbid they get in one more day of teaching before they graduate—the bottom line was my son.

As fucked up as things are between his mother and me, there's still that light. There he is, sitting on the ground, watching the older kids move on to the next school. There's my boy, hacking around with his friends while he should probably be paying attention to the speeches the alumni are giving.

But he's the reason all of this will be okay. He is here, I am here, we are here together. We will always be together, come what may— and it may indeed come.

# Doors, Throats, and Hearts

I'm staying here in the belly of the beast—the Old Greenwich house. My wife flew off to Florida to take care of her mother. Apparently, her mother needed her to fly down to trim toenails that were about an inch thick and also drive two hours to fetch some holistic pills that don't actually do anything. Pills are only available in a shack on the other side of the peninsula, run by a man with long gray hair and Birkenstock sandals. So here I am, alone for a few days with my kids, the fruits of my loin, my spawn, my offspring, the acorns that have yet to fall far from the tree. They're a lethal combination—brilliance and angst—my gift to them. The brilliance? Not so much. But certainly, I'm the architect of the gene that ensures none of us ever enjoy the moment.

But I sit here, in the quiet, when there's a break in the action, and I look up at the house my father built. The house where the echoes of my childhood still linger. But my memories don't take me back to Christmas with my parents, snow falling gently outside in December of 1978. No. They take me back, like an acid flashback, to eight months ago—August 22nd, five in the morning. Only hours after my wife had told me, flat out, that she was no longer in love with me. She told me around 2 p.m. on August 21st. My response? Rage and disbelief are the appropriate ones, I suppose.

When we arrived home, let me tell you something—that car ride

107

was something else. I packed a few things in a dramatic fashion (hey, I was committed to the performance) and stormed out, always expecting that familiar plea: "Wait! Don't go! I didn't mean it! I can't live without you!"

But it never came.

I motored over in my obscene Volvo XC90 to my friend Vinny's house. Vinny, the one I've known for what feels like my entire life, around 30 years. Vinny, the trombone player, of all things, but absolutely without question, the one I can call my brother. He called at 3 p.m. on a Monday, saying, "Come, come here now." And so I went. Though it was only afternoon, it felt like midnight. Time had no meaning; in that moment, it was as though I had crossed into Hell.

I pulled up in his driveway, told him to take me to the nearest liquor store, and he took the wheel of his opulent suburban carnival truck. We bought more alcohol than anyone could reasonably need, and I started telling him about the day's events. My best friend, who's never been fond of my wife, was quick to cut to the chase: "How are you gonna divide up the assets?"

I, still in shock, swimming in the possibility that it was really over, was suddenly hit with waves of disbelief—maybe it wasn't over, right? Seventeen years—it couldn't be, could it? I remember vividly feeling a burst of bravado, convincing myself that what had just happened was okay, even good. Finally, it was over. It had to be for the best, right? About time. It's going to be great. Then, like a sudden tidal wave of despair, I found myself running outside, ripping handfuls of Vinny's sparse lawn out of the ground with both fists. I heaved, coughed, and spit—feeling like I was dying in the purest form of anguish. I grabbed at the Earth like it was the only thing left, the only thing that would accept me. The grass, the dirt, the sky, the moon, the air, the grub worms, the oak tree helicopters. Everything around me became a symbol of a random, horrible, animalistic meltdown. I wasn't in control. The Earth let me puke myself into it, absorbing every last bit of that devastation. It was all I had left.

The grassless chunks—they exist today like an unspoken monument. Vinny doesn't know what they are, but I do. Every time I go to his house, I see them, even if they're invisible to everyone else. They are the scars of a moment, a part of the landscape now, buried beneath the grass that will inevitably grow back. But the thing is, those scars are permanent. The earth will heal, sure, but the wound that I inflicted on myself, on my soul—it's still there. Hidden, like a kidney removed, no longer visible to the world, but forever a part of me.

And that day, that night, the collapse of everything I thought I knew—it's changed me. I feel like I'm stuck in a never-ending cycle of pain like time is supposed to heal but hasn't, not for me. Maybe the healing will come, eventually. Maybe, like a broken bone that slowly knits together stronger than before, there's a future where this makes me stronger. But right now, I just feel weak. I'm like that man who walks into the hospital with back pain and discovers the cancer. Nothing will ever be the same. I won't be the person I was before. That version of me is gone, and I have to somehow rebuild, but I'm scarred. We all are. It's just how we handle the scars that define us.

So we press on, we damaged men. We try to heal, to move past the weight of it all. Some days, it works. We shake it off, put one foot in front of the other, and do what we can. On those days, it feels like we're okay. But then, there are days where everything feels suffocating—like you can't breathe like the ground is crumbling beneath your feet. You think you've hit rock bottom, only to realize there's another layer underneath, a deeper pit of despair you didn't see coming. And that's where I am now, struggling with shame, regret, self-doubt. I look back on everything that's wrong with me, with us, and it feels like an endless cycle of failure.

I wasn't good enough, not in the ways that matter. We weren't good together, not in the ways that matter. I didn't provide for my family in the way I should have. Hell, I'm not even a good cook. The one thing I've ever been good at, my friend Jake said, was being a father to my beautiful children. And in that moment, I wanted to argue—what did I really do? I wasn't even wanted. All I did was spurt into a woman's vagina. That was my contribution? What else have I done that counts?

I've made some music, sure. I've worked with artists who produced records. I can play the guitar. But what does that matter? A man's worth is measured by how much he's loved. And by that measure, I've failed. So, who does that make me? Exactly.

I spent that night with Vinny, drinking and talking about how great this was going to be, and I was finally well rid of her etc., etc. We called it at about one in the morning, and I tried to sleep in his guest bed. Uh-uh, nothin' doing. I wailed into my pillow, howled and coughed, and wailed. Thank God Vinny sleeps with earplugs, thank God. I tossed, turned, and howled for about four hours, and then I had a great idea: get in the car and go see my wife!

How I arrived there alive is a mystery to this day. Bleary-eyed, still drunk, and pathetic, I walked up the stairs to what, up until the day before was my bedroom. The room this acid trip is taking me back to. The room that used to belong to my mother and father. The room I was actually conceived in. That one. And I skulked in, and my wife was sitting up already. It was about 5 AM. I again paused for that statement that I somehow really believed was forthcoming: "Oh, thank God you're here. I love you. Don't ever leave again. I was wrong." But the pause only brought us to, "What's going on?"

WHAT'S GOING ON?

I broke down, although can something break down that is already thoroughly broken? Somehow, I figured out a way to do just that. I blathered, sobbed, and acted like a drunk man on no sleep whose wife just told him she was no longer *in* love with him. I turned around and headed back to my SUV. I like to turn the fog lights on because somehow I convince myself that by doing so, I have engaged the cloaking device, and the cops can't see me.

I managed not to make a pit stop at the police station, spend the night in a cell for DUI, and arrive back at Vinny's house with the sun coming up. I went back up to his guest room, picked up my cell, and called my wife. I remember ranting. I said something to the effect of, "You are going to break up this family so you can get your cunt rubbed by a big black cock?" It was not my finest hour, but it is one of my hours nonetheless. She was, through this whole thing, calm. A cucumber. The voice of reason. Sensible. Infuriating.

What I didn't know at the time was that she had been preparing for this moment for months. She had taken a trip to Denver to see her oldest friend, whom she had known her whole life. Her friend is separated from her husband. Surprise! This trip took place several months prior to the terrorist attack on the fire-engine-red Saab. As things start to unfold now, I'm starting to get a clearer picture of what actually transpired before, during, and after the "not in love" speech. She went to Denver to support her friend whose husband had recently moved out. Sound familiar? My wife's friend has two children, too. Hello? My wife stayed with her in a mansion that her husband bought with the money he made in Silicon Valley. That does not, however, sound familiar. Be that as it may, she and my wife sat for hours, I now understand, hour after hour, day after day, discussing her friend's situation, that I now can see my wife felt like was, in fact, her situation.

And so she made it her situation. And so now it is mine.

But I didn't have any time to prepare. I was blindsided. Nobody's fault; you can't tell someone that they should start to get ready for a breakup speech. "Take your time. When you're ready, we can have the real breakup speech, but you might want to start getting ready, you know, do some exercises, warm-ups, whatever you have to do. When you're ready, I'll break up with you. No rush, take your time." Yeah, doesn't work like that. It just happens. And there is always one person who was caught unawares. So I was, I think understandably, a bit upset. I was the yin to her yang. For every calm and calculated response, there was a more agitated and hyper-emotional question.

We would have "discussions" in the days following that would go something like, "You don't see me like a man?" Pause. Pause. "Not right now." "Not now? Did you ever?" "I don't know." "You don't *fucking* know? Did you ever *fucking* know? What the *fuck* DO you know?" Calm. Statue-like impassive face. "I know I can never live like that again."

Then I would storm out, after having re-designed the woodwork in the door to the bedroom with my fist, and I would get in the Volvo gunship and scream bloody murder until I could no longer make a sound with my ravaged larynx.

Now, back here again, almost a year later, after all of that, the door is still not repaired; I wonder if it ever will be. I wonder if I ever will be.

I hope so.

Doors, throats, and hearts. Oh, and grubworms.

# Buddy

I see faces in rugs. Little swirls and shadows in the fibers can sometimes give life to something that is hidden but there if you let yourself see it. I see these faces in Italian marble, linoleum, and, of course, clouds. But there they most certainly are; it just takes an open mind to see them. Odd patterns in trodden grass patches, stains on walls, a distortion created by a drop of water on a floor— you know, the usual. But I never was one to see the writing on the wall. Just the patterns. I fell into a really bad pattern for 15 years. So did my wife. But she saw the writing on the wall and eventually decoded it. It turns out our hieroglyphics spell out the words, "It's probably all fucking over."

Things happen for a reason, says my androgynous compadre. "Everything happens for a reason." How can that be? Did I manifest this thing to go the way of the spotted owl? And try as we may to carry on with this experiment, all the while hoping the love will come back and find its way back to its rightful owners, it doesn't. It left home and found better owners. Ones that feed it more let it sleep on the bed, brush it, walk it, and praise it when it brings back the bone.

I attended a Fourth of July fireworks display with my family. They're still my family. As the great Aimee Mann said, "What a waste of gunpowder and sky." I watched the bombs bursting in the air on the beach, directly under the star-spangled banner at half-mast (as it always is now). It was nice, ooooh, ahhhhhh. Walked my family over to THE RED SAAB and said goodnight. Five minutes later, I got a call from my kids on the cell telling me they already missed me. Yeah, that really made me feel like a man. I then headed over to a large outside party where I could have had my pick of several older gentlewomen. I don't mean to sound cocky. Again, no pun intended, I'm not irresistible; well, I'm getting there. It's just that these girls had become desperate due to divorce, a litany of strange men, and their ever-encroaching age. These particular handsome ladies had quite a bit of wear and tear on them. How sad when it is said about a woman that she is "handsome."

I went home. I sat down outside my front steps and actually had a long conversation with Buddy, my reverse-racist lawn jockey. The ever-diligent Guard of the Great Keep; View Street. I wiped him down with my hands, brushing tiny fake Caucasian paint flakes off his little head. He has funny little cat eyes, and I don't know why. He's got a red vest, a white and red cap, the two colors divided up in alternating upended triangles, green pants, and black shoes. He holds what used to be a working lantern. But that light has long since gone out. He holds it still, though. He always will until someone takes him away, breaks him, or humankind is finally snuffed out like the locusts that we are.

I sat with him, learned from him, and got strength from him. I feel like I should be carrying the lamp now. Hasn't he done enough? Isn't it time for him to rest and for me to hold the lantern that holds not a shard of an old glass bulb yet whose meaning for me has been nothing short of pure illumination? But not yet, not just yet. Please, I need more time. I need more time with the Master. I need more time to find my dignity. I need more time to stand in the rain and snow and searing heat and smile. Just like he does. I need more time to be wise, to be certain, and to be happy. Happy through my flaking paint, my failing body, and the end of my marriage. I need more time with the Master. Then I can stand strong, even looking like a carnival freak, even wearing a clown suit, and despite the fact that someone has painted on me a false face. Or was it me who did that? Whose face am I rubbing clean? Who am I trying to return to its original form? Am I rubbing him, or is it he who has been trying to reveal me to myself all along? Oh, you clever teacher. Yes, I need more time with the Master, and then, someday, I can go out into the world, stare out into the future with my strange eyes, hold my lantern and my own, flake and stand, hold and believe. Hold and survive. Hold and love once again.

# Cleaning House

M y wife is in Nashville again, business, I think. Certainly seems like it. But we never really know. And we are starting to wonder if we even care. But she called tonight, taking a moment to call her son and daughter before she couldn't be reached in a rock club. She said it was déjà vu. We met many years ago; she auditioned for my rock band 21 years ago as a background singer, with the voice of an angel, and, as it was then, looked like one, was instantly hired, and she has now been transported back in time to our humble beginnings in a rock club in Nashville. We started at clubs in New York like The Bitter End, CBBs, Kenny's Castaways, The China Club, and on and on. We did gigs at 3:30 in the morning for my father and his drunken, cigar-smoking friend. We followed metal bands that went horribly over their set and watched their large hair and fast and smart guitar riffs, and then when it was our turn to play, we sang and performed pathetically as their crowd walked out in disgust because we weren't playing Slayer. My wife and I were galvanized, baptized, and ordained on a booze-soaked stage in lower Manhattan in the late eighties.

She called me tonight from a replicated beer-soaked, oak-floored rock club in Nashville, Tennessee, and remembered and talked of our old connection, of our beginnings. For we have a beginning, we really do. There is a reason we are together, and it isn't complete bullshit. I have no idea whether or not she is flirting or dancing or fucking some guy tonight in her hotel room, and I am starting to think it really doesn't mean a fucking thing if she is. I'm starting to think that the only thing that really matters to me is that I can validate why we hooked up in the first place. And she is where we first began, and it's almost enough, almost enough to remind me that we were brothers, brothers in arms, man and wife, taking up arms against the mediocrity of eighties music. We DID have a purpose. There IS a reason we are together; we DID fight and die for something, and what do you know about that? And if she takes on some dude from Nashville tonight to get the shit fucked out of her, then what does that really mean to me? Let's see how that affects Buddy. Not a whit. So why me? Enough. Enough. Enough.

And here I am in Old Greenwich, bleaching floors and considering a steam cleaner for these carpets because, quite frankly, this place is nothing short of disgusting. I am wiping down toothpaste-spattered faucets, Tilexing toilet bowls, and drains, Windexing the microwave, Dust Busting and Swiffering the floors, cleaning up after someone else's mess, and I am suddenly not too concerned about what she may or may not be doing tonight. Did she buy the double-A batteries at Stew Leonard's yesterday for her Armageddon vibrator? I don't know; maybe she did. What does it matter to me? What good does it do for me to think about her that way? Her pleasure or her disappointment in me as a man? What good does it do for me to even think for a second about what she may or may not be doing in Nashville? It simply does not do me no good at all, and for the first time in a long time, it is really starting to matter not.

It matters not to me. How am I doing, Buddy?

Not so shabby tonight, eh, my friend?

Let me go away to sleep to wake my children with shining faces and innocent neediness. Let me awake without regret or jealous worry so I can serve up clean fruit to the hungry.

117

# Night to Queens Two

S till in Fundland, the Old Greenwich south of the village soulcage. My wife called sounding all horse, all sexed up, from Nashville, but I know it can't be from sex, can it? She said she's coming home early, which would be tomorrow instead of Thursday. She said she had nothing to do on Thursday; one has to wonder why she booked it that way. One has to wonder two things: why she is coming home early and why she sounds like a horse. My friend Simone came over; my kids love her, and she is personified by positive energy. Did I forget to mention that my arms have become numb all the time? Did I not mention this? I can't really feel my arms anymore. The reason I mention this is that Simone offered a back rub. I had so many shots at beautiful girls all my life, and I always demurred because it would cheapen her, cheapen them, and cheapen me. I took the massage, oil and all, and was struck that my torso was little more than a large male member being rubbed and lubricated by a lovely, thoughtful, and attractive woman. That sounded condescending; she is physically beautiful but, for some reason, not compelling to me sexually, even though she meets me all the way intellectually. This is my pattern. Done this all my life. Passed on a plethora of wonderful sexual experiences based on what some feminists would call, and as Simone would call, an evolved male mentality. But I'm pretty sure that in that blender of psychobabble, one would need to add the simplest ingredient, the salt of the mind:

fear.

What's wrong with a man who doesn't see the future or read some vision of the part he plays in it being right or wrong, making a moral difference? Does it matter? Not having sex with the girls I went to Europe with when I was eighteen as a musical director to their dance troupe, yet snuggling with most of them in their sleeping bags well into the sunset, make me righteous or even, quite frankly, feel what could even be remotely construed as evolved? What difference would any of this make if I had fucked each and every one of them? Did I make a difference by showing compassion and restraint? And here I am, on the phone with the woman I have been married to for 17 years, having given permission to have sex with someone else (Oh, did I fail to mention that tidbit?). Yeah, I did that in an email two weeks ago. I couldn't eat for days; here I am, listening to her voice, sounding to me very much post-coitus, having just received an erotic massage from Simone, and all I could think about was my wife with someone else. I didn't say anything, of course. I'm cool, right?

I excused myself for a minute in the guise of getting a beer in the ugly black fridge in the garage to call my wife and tell her that, hey, it was OK if she had just made love to a strange man, but that I did, in fact, need only one thing: the facts, the truth, the skinny.

"Nothing could be farther than the truth."

"Look, it's OK if you did."

"I know it's OK, but I didn't."

"OK, it's OK if you did. I just need the truth."

"That's the truth."

"OK, again, it's OK if you did…"

"I know."

"You know, it's just that you're all horse and shit."

"I don't know what that is, but I am starting to feel a bit nasally."

119

"You OK?"

"Yeah, just want to come home."

"OK, get some sleep, or are you going to a club tonight?"

"No, I'm lonely here, no friends."

"OK, call me before you get on the plane."

"OK"

"Night."

"Night."

That was it. What was that, though?

I had some banter with Simone, some really good banter; she is intuitive and damaged, just my kind of girl, but finally, she left at about 1 AM. And then, I made the old walk upstairs to the relic of the marriage bed where I used to live. But there is no cold coming off this Queen mattress, for the maker of cold is not here. But what is here is my old life. It seems like I'm visiting a museum. There is the painting I made for my wife years ago for Christmas, a brilliant and masculine portrait of a hidden-to-the-eyes corpse buried deep in a Garden of Delights, its title. Aren't I cheery? Haven't I always been? But it hangs directly across our/her bed. I joked once about taking it to View Street, and she said, to my pleasure, "It's mine."

I will try to sleep, if I can, in our/her queen bed in this room built for us. I might as well be in a Holiday Inn. This is not my room; this is not my bedroom. My bedroom sits 3 miles away in a place called Chickahominy. Buddy guards it for me now as I try to fall asleep in a strange room. I am changed, transformed, and lost. How queer it is that I called this my bedroom for ten years. It never was. I'm sorry, I'm so sorry. I am gone from here, but my imprint lives on. This plush and sexless chamber holds the key to our futile quest. This is your room now, not mine, not ours, yours.

I love you, honey. Maybe I should paint you another picture.

# The Wizard of Id

My wife is on her way back from a business trip. She had a meeting with a powerhouse guy who is going to use her connections in the music business and broker deals between artists and advertisers. Big artists. Big money. If the first deal goes through, it could mean $250,000.00 to $500,000.00 bucks in commission for her if it happens. But neither she nor I have ever been this close to something of that financial magnitude.

It should be a good thing, right? In great part, we are separated because I stopped making money, in great part because of the demise of the music business, and in an even greater part because I got depressed and lazy. So, if she makes a killing, why would she want to share it with me? She will claim to want to and even believe that herself, perhaps. But we know the truth; me sucking off that pile would be tantamount to recidivism. I would be a repeat offender. I feel terrible.

You know something is afoul when good news gives birth to dark sadness. It's like I live in opposite land. During the worst of our times, I feel good because I am in my element: misery. But in the best of times, I self-transport into regret and shame. So that's what this is: shame.

Shame on me.

This is me on shame: Shame is terrible. Terrible is a big word. From the Latin *terribilis*. Terror. These days that has its own connotation. A small group of nut jobs usurped a word. They commandeered it. But it fits what they do, and it fits what I feel. Shame is debilitating. I am terrified of feeling it for the rest of my life. I am most terrified, however, of it being what people remember me for.

Shame presupposes you can't make good on those in front of whom you shamed yourself. Even if the worst-case alcoholic turns his life around and becomes the best-case entrepreneur, he will forever still feel shame about the people he stole from, puked on, lied to, and begged from. He can never get those days back, those days that were gouged from an old tree some ne'er-do-well carved the word "fuck."

That patch of bark is gone forever, the protective layer. And for the rest of that tree's life and for the rest of that drunk's life, and for the rest of my life, there will be the emotional evidence of this unwholesome incision. Or, to be more accurate, there will be a scar, a disfigurement, a slash, a permanent decussate. I know for a fact that you can't put back on a tree that has been ripped from it. I am a damaged tree, a cut tree, but I cut myself, don't you know, I am a tree from the magical loam-fed forests on the outskirts of Oz, who cuts himself. I am a magical tree, A SELF-MUTILATING ELM!

The Scarecrow wouldn't know what to do with me; neither would the Cowardly Lion or the Tin Man. Unfortunately, if I had enough time with Dorothy, I would have liked to go on a hot air balloon ride with her. I know the Wizard can give you things like bravery, a heart, or a brain, but do you think he could take away bad things, like shame? I tell you now, I would brave a gaggle of Flying Monkeys if he could do that for me.

"If I only had no shame." De doot de doodly doot. (Sung to the tune "If I only had a brain")

# Her Feet

When my daughter cries, she looks exactly like I do when I cry; the front teeth protrude, the lower jaw recedes, we make a grimace, and we let go. She is definitely mine. In fact, she is definitely me. When she cries, I see me, and when I cry, I see her. What bond is this, crafted from pain? What explanation can there be, be it from the physicists or the social behavioral assholes or the arrogant, bought-off scientists, that we cry the same? She is me, and I am her, and we cry the same. All of a sudden, crying isn't lonely; it's a beautiful and heart-wrenching dance between father and daughter.

I miss her tonight, my partner in pain; I miss her every night, her little pounding footsteps running into our bedroom announcing the fact that she has to go pee-pee. I miss her so much. I miss her so very fucking much. The bigger picture is that working towards a healthy lifestyle, as it were, is exacting a tremendous price, as it turns out. I can't hear her little footsteps, which, as it turns out, are music to my ears, even at 3 AM in the morning. I have lost the music of her little pounding feet. I love her feet. I miss her feet. I am dying from the lack of her little pounding feet. God help me. Let me kiss her natty, silky hair in the middle of the night, assuring her, loving her, being a father to her in the only real sense of the word: father.

I'm not there anymore; won't she suffer from that? Aren't I? I hate this. I hate this so much. I miss her feet.

123

# Becoming Done

A nd so, if the absence of my daughter's two-and-a-half-inch pitter-pattering feet is the overture, then my wife's oblivion is the first and most foreboding act in this tragedy. She went out with her girlfriends last night and came back drunk. She used to have a scotch or, God forbid, two and then lean over the table and start Frenching me. I, being the child of a mother whose judgmental social frown is nothing short of a debilitating indictment of couth when you don't place your fork "tips down" after you're done eating, am a bit reticent to swap spit in a public booth. I wish I weren't, and maybe I'm not now, but I have felt the scorn of the pilgrims my whole life. It could explain my "hesitating" behavior in bed. Only with her, though.

I used to make booty calls to a beautiful girl named Lynn back before I was married. These calls were made at insane hours, always after 2 AM. She would always grant my proffer, and I would arrive, often barely prior to the crack of dawn, and she would stand at the top of her stairs, in her father's house, in a towel, wet from a shower, and hungry for me. I would jump the steps two at a time until I reached the top landing, desperate for her, and we would make love for hours. One night, I had to crawl home, literally, because of my aching colon (the organ responsible for semen, the sixth orgasm, literally a spit of air and sawdust), and we made love effortlessly, perfectly, and completely. With my wife, it has always been a tiring effort. An ill fit, an obligating, nagging wish for something more. We tried, God knows we tried. But it comes out, like that night out with her friends.

I reached into my old, tattered bag of bravery and decided to kiss her goodnight before I retreated to my little bungalow on the south side. I leaned down to kiss her, remembering her scotch kisses, her wet, sloppy, open-mouth kisses, the essence of her Brooklyn trailer park upbringing, and she actually talked it through. I said, "SHE TALKED THROUGH A KISS." Lynn, where are you? Where are you, Lynn? I left, in the bird of prey (cloaking on), and sped carelessly to the Westin Hotel in Stamford where my man/woman friend was staying. On the way, I screamed my throat out. I have learned you can kill a throat. You can annihilate it. Good to know.

I didn't have what could be considered a traditional throat anymore. What I had was a bunch of hanging, fleshy shards. By the time I arrived, ten minutes at the most, I had completely lost my voice. Jake, my good friend, listened to my whispers of rage and despair and offered some sage advice: she is gone, maybe she was never there, I don't know, but she isn't there now, she is vapor, a wisp, a shadow. She is the God of unawareness. She is pure oblivion. I reach to touch her, and I recoil as if holding a finger to a block of ice. I am reduced, like a sauce from Rachel Ray.

But wait, on second thought, have I been reduced, or do I reside in the steam rising from the quagmire? Do I want to be the result of reduction, or do I want to leave the pot of mediocrity to be sucked into the fan, which, ultimately, gets blown outside? OUTSIDE. Yes. Outside. That sounds good. That sounds right. Suck me in and blow me out. Out to the unknown, out to possibility. The filters are always moderately clogged. Who cleans their filters on anything? So it takes time to get out, but over time, as you wait your turn in the line of steam and oil, the aggressive lingering of garlic and despair, you will eventually, as long as you let go of the edge of the pot, where you will inevitably cake, you will get your chance to go out. To get out. To climb to where there's free air and cling to something beautiful, something new, for as long as you want, until you want to go again, like a fluttering, spasmodic butterfly, and you give yourself permission to go, and you keep going, born from the sauce, but free from the fear of leaving the pot.

You are also free of some other things too. Companionship, comfort, the feeling of having a wingman, that someone's got your back, and the biggest loss: sex. (Although the pedestrian and pedantic irony is that during marriage, you never had it anyway.) I often watch birds, bugs, and sad little animals that wander around all day utterly alone, looking for scraps of food, wandering aimlessly, and doing their own thing without a trace of companionship or communication. All day, just walking around, flying around, nobody loves them, nobody gives a shit where they are going or where they have been.

No, Mrs. Slug nagging Mr. Slug, "Where were you? I told you to slither home before five! Did you go on that hot sidewalk again?" There is no one wondering where they are. They don't seem to mind, so why should I? Why do I desperately want to walk up the stairs to where my wife is taking a shower and get in it with her with a bottle of baby oil? Jesus Christ, I wish I could fly away and go bob up and down on a random tree branch and clean my feathers and think about nothing. Especially not her. Yes, to fly away, to soar, and to leave all this despair behind. I want to take my son and my daughter, take their hands, and fly like Peter Pan to another place. A place fraught with danger but safe from a cold and bitter soon-to-be ex-wife. No, nothing's official, and no one's talking about it, but judging from a conversation we had yesterday in which she clearly indicated that the chances of us having sex again were abysmal due to an inability on her part to find me even remotely sexy, because, as she said and has said on many occasions, seemingly with a hidden glee, that it was never good. So how could it ever be? Point taken. I get it.

No sex. Ever. Done. And I finally realized the real truth of this thing: she's done, it's done, and now, I have to... start... becoming... done.

# Lords of the Ring

I wake up, and I guess you could call it waking up; it's more of a transition from a nightmarish dream state to a waking sadness, and I have to pop a 20 mg Aciphex to control my burning out-of-control stomach acids. Lately, I have to, at some point in the day, pop a Lorazepam, 0.5 mg (substituted for Ativan), for nerves. Mild, you understand, not an antidepressant, just a little thing to keep me from hitting walls or dropping to my knees from sadness. I take this sporadically. But then, after dinner, I take Diovan, 80 mg, for my high blood pressure, and at the end of the night, I take Simvastatin, 20 mg, substituted for Zocor for cholesterol. I keep this personal pharmacy in a tin from Czech Airlines that my wife brought back from one of her stints to one of the promised lands.

She thinks Europe is better in every way; let's see, she needs an appendectomy in Prague. But here's what I don't have to take: a wife who doesn't love me anymore because what used to be called my wife still loves me, and we may be the only couple I know right now that isn't enduring permanent self-induced resentment. Nobody is having sex, not married, so I can't say that we had to give that up; it wasn't there anyway. It's just that we stopped pretending that someday it would start again. The married pretended it would get better; we did until the lie became more obvious than the delusion. The truth killed delusion. K.O. Hold her hands up in the air, declare her the victor, and

127

let me hold her, her sweat mixing with red satin, and tell her how proud I am of her. Let me hoist the chair, place it in the ring for her to sit on, take out her teeth guard, pour streaming water from a bottle into her mouth, and say, "You did good out there." Give me a butterfly band-aid; she's got a cut over her eye. Give me a towel; I want to drape it over her tired, sweating shoulders, and let me walk her to the back room where she can shower and rest. As for me, not quite the victor at this particular time, I continue to do stupid things, like, for example, put it on.

Tonight, for no reason whatsoever, I put it on. A single ring of white gold that she, with her little shaking hands, slid onto my reticent left-hand ring finger so many years ago. But she did it. She slid it on; it was the same round metal object. It is the original. The same piece of metal that I wore as I broke plaster, hammered nails into two-by-fours, gouged gunk from pipes, fed cable through ceilings, hung insulation, shoveled snow, dug ditches, masturbated, swam in the Mediterranean, raked my sweating hair, brushed my teeth, played hundreds of thousands of notes on the guitar, piano, and bass, let the sand in the Roman Coliseum fall through my fingers, wiped my ass, bathed my son, wiped his ass, my daughter's ass, even my wife's ass after her episiotomy. It's the same piece of metal that held my son's hands down as I let them cut the flesh off his one-day-old penis, and it has remained on my finger for good or ill for seventeen years. It's the ring that Hope built. And for no reason at all, I put it on tonight.

I went into the clubhouse within the clubhouse, the room within a room in View Street, a discreet little closet created out of what the fuck else can we do with this architectural mistake little space behind the door in the bedroom; where I house our two rings, on a sterling silver strand with a dog tag demarcating our wedding date, and I put it on.

And here is the punch line: it comforts me. Like you can't believe this still-shining, much to my surprise, for I thought when the love dies, the shine will die, but it still shines. It shines and comforts me.

So, guess what? I'm gonna sleep with this on. I'm gonna let this ring of white gold that she put on me comfort me. I was gonna throw both these things in the Byram River, at the same location where I asked her to marry me, but now I realize I can't do it. I can't let go of this shiny little circle of naïve hope, this little trinket of innocence, of our idea of love, fucked and ridiculous and flawed and wrong and misguided and mistaken and so horribly ill-conceived, born from, on both of our parts, fear. Because it's not its fault, I can't throw it to the dogs. It's been there the whole time. It's been trying to tell me, this silly little metal ring, to love her, to honor her, and to be a man worthy of wearing such a powerful symbol. And I ignored it, her and me. I still don't believe in marriage, but I believe in this ring on my finger: scratched, boiled, frozen, oiled, soiled, bent, disregarded, forgotten, covered, bandaged for surgery, revealed, reviled, relished. I, for some reason, feel like it is my old friend, so I'm gonna wear it tonight, and it's going to be there when I wake up tomorrow. Like it always used to be.

It still shines so brightly. Can you believe it?

# The Events of Last Night

And so, I, without further ado, recount the events of last night: I returned from the strip club, Beamers, and I had many lap "dances" from very many beautiful women. They aren't uninteresting women by any stretch (again, no pun intended). Almost all were from the Eastern Bloc; one was studying to be a forensic scientist, and one was a budding physical therapist. All of them were strikingly beautiful. I do well with women when I want to, and it was good, clean, and fun. But after a while, there was no difference between the way they smelled and the way I smelled. I was encrusted with glitter. Enough said.

So, I got in the soccer mom bird of prey and headed home to Buddy. I, for the first time (and may I say I now fully support this phenomenon), sat in the hottest water my heater could muster. I sat, I say, in the shower. My arms and legs are now completely numb; I am broken and broken.

The woman's body is a wonder, a miracle, a universe. They are never to be truly discovered; they are the true enigma, the Promised Land, the unattainable. God's gift and curse. I felt paradise, rapture, and desire, found Utopia five minutes at a time, and then rushed home to sit in a hot shower for as long as my heating unit could deliver the cleansing water to me, on me, and, in a way, inside me.

I don't know what any of this means; I feel I am a slowing locomotive whose engineers still throw in the coal, but to no avail – the engine is tired, dog-tired, and done. But the crew will try until they need to abandon their loyal, fallen beast of burden because it carried them for so long; they owe it to it. And it, in some existential way, the dying motor loves them back and gives all it can through the aching wheels, the nerve-dead legs, and the overall debilitating futility of its very purpose.

# Lament of a Home Dad

---

Somebody, please tell me I'm a good father. I have never had a job; my job was to write music and play it for people for tips. And then my job became them – I have given everything to them, all of me, to the detriment of myself. Now, I wonder what I have done.

In this hedonistic Mecca, I have been made to feel like a bug. These money-grubbing, cozen people have wounded me for good. I have been so poisoned to my marrow that I can't relieve myself of the stigmatizing effects of capitalist success. Would my son be better off if I had a job every day and came home in shiny black leather Kenneth Cole shoes, in a dry-cleaned Etro shirt with a Prada tie – wrapped like a sick hedge fund action figure in a Giorgio Armani suit? A vision of stability? Wait, never mind – I would rather die.

And so I may.

# And Bingo Was
# His Name Oh

I'm starting to unravel. The numbness in my arms and legs is getting untenable. It's constant. I yelled at the beast last night, informing her that I was, in fact, breaking up with her. It's from a *Seinfeld* episode. I am sick of feeling like a loser ex-husband. I don't want to do this anymore.

I have had the kids for the last four days and nights because my wife has been in the studio with a famous female songwriter who is best known for her ability to "anticipate." I've had no time to recharge. So I snapped. I don't want to make her feel better all the time anymore. I want to feel better.

She scheduled Bingo Night for "the family" tonight at our swim club in Stamford. BINGO NIGHT. Ladies and gentlemen, I implore you—how the fuck am I going to get through this? Add to this delicious bouillabaisse the special ingredient of my parents coming for THREE WEEKS to stay in the extra bedroom. My father can't even walk; he sprained an ankle that is already 2 inches in diameter from his degenerative nerve disease. I don't want to be around anybody. I just want a do-over. I want to go back. I want her never to coerce me into marrying her.

She wanted to marry this lunatic artist songwriter asshole, suspiciously enough, three weeks after I was offered a publishing deal with Geffen Music. Coincidentally, I had just announced I was purchasing my father's house in Byram. (It's not the Old Greenwich house, but a small saltbox not far from Chickahominy.)

Come to find out, the sex for her was never that good. Was it for me? I don't know; I'm an idiot male. I pump. But for her to enter into this thing from the beginning—unbeknownst to me—feeling that the other is inadequate is unforgivable. Then, to continue the farce and add to this mix of tomfoolery, a kid? Then, as the whole thing starts to fall apart, all the while petrifying like ancient wood, to go ahead and HAVE ANOTHER ONE?

I know. I'm culpable. I colluded. I know.

But aren't they supposed to know better? I guess they don't know anything more than anyone else. I guess we're all on our own. And now, I have to suck it up, act like nothing happened, "I'm good, how're you doin'?" and go to fucking Bingo.

So it's off to Roxbury Swim and Tennis Club! We're meeting the McGoverns, an interesting couple. He is an established builder in our little opulent hamlet and is 65. She, a coquettish 48, has had scads of surgery, not for ill health, but rather because of an ill temperament for aging. He already had his family and, in fact, two 30-something-year-old children. But these two found each other somehow after he divorced and sent his original kids off to the world. But Lindsay and Robert McGovern found out they couldn't conceive. So they adopted. One, two, and then the sibling of two was born and offered up to the buyers of two. Apparently, this woman keeps having children and giving them up, and the McGoverns, to their credit, wanted the siblings together, even though they didn't want another, so good for them. The problem is, three kids for a 65-year-old man is, well, a big fat fucking problem.

Imagine chasing around a toddler at that age. I mean, the youngest is two on top of a 5-year-old and a 9-year-old. All adopted. I think the reason the woman gave up her babies is because her baby's father is on crack. The kids sure act like it. But then, their father is so dog-tired he can't deal with it. And she, well, as much as I like her, is, well, nuts. Face, neck, arms, legs, stomach, ass. All tucked or sucked. The teeth are so white they're blue, and the skin is so artificially tanned that it's orange leather. And my wife has befriended this most unlikely of soul mates and yet, of course, the most likely. Lindsay told my wife recently that she and Robert haven't fucked in three years. I was telling a friend this recently, and he said, "I can beat that. My first wife and I went without sex for four and a half years!"

My God, what in the world? The more I talk to people about their marriages, the more stunned I am that so many people do it and keep doing it.

So, at Bingo – and let me just state for the record that I fucking hate Bingo – I mean, I just fucking hate it. If that's what you do when you get older, then just kill me now, because if that's old age – sitting with a square of cardboard and movable opaque red plastic number covers – then I would rather be dead. I would rather be dead without Bingo than be alive with it.

So there we were all nine of us: their kids – a nightmarish result of skittish genes and far too indulgent adoptive parents – and us, my family, my perfect children, and my odd and damaged wife. I had brought a six-pack, Lindsay had brought vodka, and I was enjoying the healing power of cold beer and vodka cranberry. It went, as Bingo does; my son won quite a cornucopia of candy, and my daughter won some bubbles. Lindsay kept touching my arm – you know, how they do – and laughing hysterically at just about everything I was saying.

I couldn't help but think that Robert when he wasn't seemingly nodding off to sleep, was bothered by this. He, as I mentioned, is a builder, and I guess he makes quite a good living. At one point,

Lindsay asked if we could get her family into the club. I, of course, inquired if that meant they were prepared to leave their other club – a pretentious series of buildings with a pool and a four-star restaurant on the cove in Greenwich. She said no, they'd just be members of both.

I then made a delightful comment about how she's got to start taking it easy lest the well dry up. She looked at me, puzzled, then turned to her husband, who looked back at her with an expression very much resembling Lurch from _The Addams Family_. She looked right at him and said, without a large amount of humor, "The well better not fucking dry up."

He bent his head down and went to see if he had B13 – Bingo.

# Letter To My Wife Never Sent

I don't know what I would do without you. The very thought of you not being there is debilitating and truly terrifying. I have never told you this, and I still haven't; I couldn't face another day without knowing you were on the other end of the phone.

To never again see your shining, amazing, most beautiful face, dimples, green eyes, and true, true, true, true, true, true, true love, your smile – a smile no one else will ever see, I now know in my heart of hearts, will ever know but me – to never see that again would be the end. The end of me.

The very thought of the loss of you puts me into a panic beyond my formidable comprehension. But you are there, more than ever, so I go on another day. You have to stay here in this world, or I will collapse, disintegrate, dry up, and die. I am becoming numb and hopeless, but I am hanging on because I will see you another day. After all is said and done, I absolutely could not live without you.

I'll talk to you tomorrow.

# I Am Become Father

I received an unheard-of email from my partner in marital crime. It was unprecedented. It said, after a rather lengthy preamble representing a desire on her part for me not to think for a second that this would change anything in any manner, shape, or form and that our current situation was under no circumstances likely to change anytime soon. (You got that right); that she missed me.

Now, ladies and gentlemen of the jury, I must again implore you. How does one respond to something like that with such stipulation and self-protection? I felt like I was reading the Surgeon General's warning on the side of a pack of Marlboros. Can I really enjoy the smoke now? Could it possibly taste as good as without the conditions? Of course not. "This means nothing, really, but I miss you." This, my friends, is a microcosm of my relationship with my better half.

"Sex is no good, marry me." "I love your creativity, it's what attracted me to you, go get a fucking job." "I don't like this house anymore. Let's renovate it." "I like it now. Get out." "Get out of this house your father built." Speaking of my father, my parents arrived yesterday for three weeks. They are staying in the guest room.

I love my parents. I come from my father. He gave me my gift to relate to the Christian hedgie, to the Irish plumber, to the Mexican laborer. I'd better get used to relating to Mexican laborers - I'd better get used to doing it in Spanish soon. *Sí*. I have friends so varied in style, background, and personality that it confounds my wife. And I am close to them all, on a deep level. I can't relate to any other stratum. What's the point? My father gave me that, my most precious attribute, my secret weapon. He is loved by so many but is, I fear, a burden to my mother, the saint. I know she wouldn't trade him in for all the Scotch in Scotland, but it wears at her, I know. He is all-consuming. Am I? He is hobbling around with a ski boot brace and an aluminum cane. He loves me more than life; so does she. It occurs to me they must love me like I love my kids. Scary. And I will be looked at with pity by them someday? It's the natural course, I guess. I hate people who, when I say I don't want to get old, say, "It beats the alternative." I hate those pat little "I don't want to think about it" phrases. Let's talk about the alternatives! Is there a way to do life and not become the very thing that you so desperately do not want to become? There has to be! What about the old in Tuscany? They are revered, aren't they? Don't they live out their lives with their families, playing checkers in the sun with friends, drinking casks of the local wine? Didn't Frances Mayes tell us that? If they can be respected, as opposed to the seething disrespect of American culture towards their old, then maybe getting old would be tolerable.

Do you know what else they do there? The Italian women let their husbands have a *domina*, a mistress - they call them *gumadas*. They even go as far as reserving Friday nights for them. It's known and accepted, and it keeps the family together. But it's done purposely, from and for tradition. Here in the *Estados Unidos*, we resist and resist and resist and resist the possibility that there may be a better way. Speaking of that, *México*, I mean, the Latin culture, also does what the Italians do - they stay together and have a Chiquita on the side. They are much more family-oriented than the traditional white Christians. Perhaps the invasion will bring Americans to their senses.

I always preferred olive skin, anyway.

# I Hope My Parents
# Don't Read This

S ome days are earmarked for sadness. It seems to me there is some schedule I am unaware of that dictates what will be a good day and what will be a terrible day. I think there must be a cosmic schedule. I don't want to see it, though - would you? It would include the day the love died, the day you found out you had breast cancer, or the day you realized your parents were closing in on death.

The calendar of the future, if you could glance at it, would have a date on it when you watched your aging father hobble to a chair and ask for his scotch refilled for hours on end - unending hours. There would be a date and time on this calendar when you first realize your mother more closely resembles your grandmother, an aging, decaying relic holding on because of a nonexistent alternative; she is confused and tired.

Most disturbingly, however, is watching her in servitude to a more immediate victim: her time-ravaged betrothed. My father, the icon, is literally fading away before my eyes, shrinking, drinking, and waiting. Playing out his hand. Playing the cards he was dealt? No, I think not. He did not choose wisely. He gave up too soon. He waited to see what was around the corner instead of choosing which corner he wanted to turn.

I love him, I love my father, I love my mother, but I can't repeat them. I can't be like them. They sit, commiserate, and go over the day's events. What events? They drink Cutty Sark by the gallon and talk about - I can't imagine what.

I can't be like them, or like the old me for that matter. I am a reeling vessel in space with no connection whatsoever to what or where I'm supposed to be. I am Major Tom, lost in space. I'm the chimp stabbing at a short-circuited control panel. I'm waiting out my air supply in my strapping white and orange space suit, running out of $O_2$, running out of answers, running out of the will to live.

Let me go gracefully, though - not like the elderly, not like the common folk, not like a shadow with a bottle of air, a plastic mask on my face, a diaper on my torso, iron wheels with rubber tires, and a colostomy bag like a spoiler in the back. Let me not lead me to the fiscally prudent, brown-tinted macaroni and cheese in the cafeteria of the assisted living halfway house to inevitability. Save me, Jesus? I wish. Save me, me.

But how? How?

# The Date

Took her out tonight. You know who. I debated it, but I've come to find out that she likes to have a nice time – a time to rest the mind and heart and just enjoy the simple pleasure of the company of a friend, which is apparently what I am now. Fitting – it's how we began.

But still, I took her to the Crab Shell. As you may imagine, it's on the water. They have crabs, in or out of the shell. We got a pedestrian table surrounded by loud Khakis and too-tanned husband bait. So, for the very first time in my life, I greased the maître d' to get a quiet table right on the water. And so I did it with my shaking, nerve-damaged hands. I acted like Robert Vaughn and palmed a twenty. I got the table I wanted right there on the damn water. For her. Or for me? Was it for her to start thinking about me as a man who, for the first time, is taking care of her like men do? Don't know – will never know – but I did it, and I'd do it again. She never knew, and would it matter?

These events go by every day with such meaning to one of us and so little meaning for the other that it makes me wonder if there is a connection at all. With every disconnect, my limbs go more and more numb. It's gotten to the point where I had to make an appointment to get an MRI, a magnetic resonance imaging machine – the huge plastic tube you crawl into for half an hour and go deaf from the clacking, and you hang on a minute by minute, trying with all your might not to scream, jump out, and find a grassy opening. I've never had one, but I've heard it's not fun. I've messed myself up in the head so bad that my body is so twisted with knots, and my nerves have been so squeezed by stress and self-induced emotional trauma as to restrict blood flow to my limbs.

Aren't I adorable? Aren't I just the picture of an irresistible male? Holy shit, I wouldn't want me either. But we had a nice time – talking about what, I don't know. I just know it was rather bereft of controversy; it was a nice time. Did I mention it was a nice time? Nice – what a loaded word. As defined in the Bible – by which I mean Webster's – pleasant or enjoyable, kind, or showing courtesy, friendliness, or consideration. Example: "It was a nice gesture to return the money." I just report it, folks – I don't make this up.

So we had this time – I guess it fits the definition – and we left the Crab Shell on the water to go to the actual water – the beach. And we sat and talked about what I don't remember until she attacked my father.

He represents the villain here to her – the possible cause of how I let her take care of me the way my father has let my mother take care of him. I get it – I see the similarity – any idiot would – he contracted a debilitating disease, but not as debilitating as he would have us believe, perhaps. He did do an awful lot of blue fishing those days but couldn't do the laundry while my mother was at work. In other words, he embellished. And he let my mother carry the load like I did with my wife – without a debilitating disease, of course.

But wait – here's the thing: as she equated me to him or blamed him for what was wrong with us, I realized something – that's my damn father you're talking about – cool it. Until you have walked in his crippled shoes, you can't know – so maybe you should shut it. When was the last time you had your neck fused? Are you on so much medication from the pain that you can't think straight? Eh? Blame me – not him. Let's not forget how damaged you yourself are. Let's not forget how damaged we all are, with all the bullshit we carry from all the bullshit our parents innocently imparted into us – all our regret, secret shame, and utter bullshit. Tons of it – our hearts teeming with faults and subterfuge.

My wife judging my father is like the sparrow with a broken back calling the half-eaten, twitching finch lame.

Enough.

Had a nice time, though – nice.

# The Town Employee

I've lit my children like fireworks. They're lit, going, sparkling, and glowing. They will shower this soul-dead world with light; they will try to give light in the fog of duds.

They're going. I lit the fuses, and they won't go out now – it's too late. The fire's too hot. My little Roman candles. They're on their way up; look at them go. I've done my job. I am the guy with the punk stick; I'm done, my lungs are filled with creosote, my hands are caked with gunpowder and burned from flash marks. But look at them go. Look at them – aren't they beautiful? I did that; you couldn't see them if not for me.

This is what they should say about this little man who tended the rockets, who ran around in a yellow slicker and uncomfortable galoshes:

Husband/Father

He let her go; she's free.

He lit them, and they're beautiful glowing bursts of pure sparkly fire, going up and up and up.

Fly free. Shine.

Please don't ever forget the guy in the trenches running around like an idiot with one purpose: to light you, to make you hot, like human fire – to rise. Once you have, I can sit down, drink a cold beer, and stop hating myself.

I need so badly to sit down with the other fire starters if there are any – there must be; I just can't see them in the dark yet – but if they're there, we'll laugh. My God, how I need to laugh again. But how I do enjoy watching you light makers explode and rise.

It's why I'm here, I think, and I like the log our kind sits on – it's a good log. Fallen but sturdy, snapped but still useful – serving its purpose, just like me.

# Macaroni and the Blood of Christ

W hat makes a good lover? I'm not entirely sure I know. I think at my best, I was with Lynn, my twenty-year-old nympho. But what made that good? Well, that she was a nympho was a very, very good start. She would look at my arms – my sleeves rolled up – and get turned on, like a man gets turned on by glancing at a woman's thigh, so it does exist.

But when we made love, it was crazy. I loved her skin, her hair, her face, her unbelievable body, her dark, oval eyes, her everything except her *self*. That was a snag. She was terribly damaged, which works for a while, and then the damage rubs off on you. Then you become part of her damage, and then, well, you take your hackneyed prostate and go home.

I look back now and wonder: Did I ever have the scene on the beach? The breathless, sand-sprinkled, oil-skin, ocean-dappled, heart-stopping kiss? No. I did not.

I never wanted to get married, but I had received the ultimatum, and out of fear of losing the "love of my life," I agreed to this absurd concept of coupling for the rest of my life with just one person. And so, the minister read his - I'd rather say, his "rhetoric" - we faked smiles, and presto! We were like all that had come before.

And many who had once stood on threadbare, Christ-approved, commercial-grade red carpet runners, leading up the three absurdly wide steps to the magical, mystical pulpit - like a sacred voodoo priestess soapbox that you have strangely been given permission to visit - watched as we, the latest commoners granted the temporary right to stand where normally only the mouthpieces of the Gods can stand, said our "vows." We stood as all couples who have given in to this most tenacious of traditions have stood. Where men in white robes and purple scarves spout mystical rhetoric, drink the likeness of blood, always mumbling, kissing silver cups, and making symmetrical hand gestures, usually stand and receive the apparent "blessings" of the "Lord" to stay together, whether we wanted to or not.

Tangent Alert.

When the shit hit the fan, and I was summarily dismissed on August 21 of last year - a Monday - I created in my head an imaginary old Italian woman sitting on my shoulder the whole time, yelling at me, saying:

"Whatsa matta fa you? You think anybody is happy?" She then slaps me across the back of my head.

"You gotta make this work, you promised. You keep a promise. You don't leave. You made your promise in front of God and family, and you find a way to make her happy, and she finds a way to make you happy, and you raise you children, and sit with them, and teach them, and love them, and honor your whole family, and THAT is what you gonna do."

Her eyes burn into me; she is close, smells like garlic, and is shaking. Her skin is a coffee-stained road map. She is wise, she is old, and she is most probably right.

In my mind's eye, I kiss her on her cheek; it feels like leather on my lips, and go tell my wife I love her, and I call the kids in for dinner - pasta with gravy, fresh zucchini, and a side of having honored my commitment - and we sit down, say our prayers of thanks to God for our beautiful family, and we eat.

But it didn't exactly go that way.

(End Tangent)

After having said the perfunctory words that, like a secret password, get you into a tree house, we walked back down the ridiculously wide steps, down off the forbidden place – the place of blessed water, holy chalices, and big old dusty books filled with commands and rules and twisted subterfuge for the masses, words designed to intimidate, confuse, and sublimate. We walked slowly and carefully, lest the bride have an embarrassing moment tripping on her train, down these steps of chagrin.

Steps designed to make the common man want to prostrate himself in awe and raw self-flagellation, steps leading to the place where only the sanctified can inhabit – because you see, it's the house of God, and whatever they say, goes; how can it not? Stand up to them? I think not. Did you know they are starting to put ATMs in churches? For offerings?

Offerings?

Holy bilking, Batman!

So we made our way down the linen-lined runner covering the Christ-approved carpet, which, apparently, is not good enough for the sanctity of marriage. We stepped carelessly over tossed roses and rice and strode slowly but mindful of the natural creases in the disposable satin-like fabric – or do they reuse it? We walked back down the aisle past all our friends and family and into the sunlight.

Or did we push open the big oak doors strewn with crucifixes into complete darkness?

Only Bella Nona knows for sure.

# What's with the Clint Eastwood References?

My wife and I arrived in Bermuda for our honeymoon 17 years ago. I had wrapped a gram of coke in several layers of Glad Wrap, a fitting product name for its purpose, I thought, and I stuffed it down with a pencil into a Curel lotion bottle. I find Curel to be the most soothing and least greasy of body lotions. For my face, I prefer Oil of Olay.

Did I mention I was gay? We stepped into the oppressive heat of the island, into customs, and I saw something I will never forget. THEY WERE CHECKING LOTION BOTTLES. What is the matter with me? Do I think I'm so fucking clever that I'm the only one who would think of this sophomoric smoke and mirrors scheme? Apparently, I was not. It is or was common practice to harbor illegal powders and dried cannabis plants inside lotion bottles. Of course, there is lotion in the bottles, but the Bermudian custom agents were digging in with little wires - wires designed to dig into lotion bottles that belonged to staggering idiots.

This was the first time I really felt like my wife, and I were in something together. My first thought was that she was going home. Let me say I would have, and still would, go down for her. I would have taken the rap, the Glad Wrap, as it were. I at least know that about myself: that beautiful little soul isn't going down. My soul, well, it ain't so beautiful - I would have survived.

But it occurs to me that I would, but for the grace of whatever, still be in Bermuda, but not at the Sonesta Beach and Resort Hotel, but rather an unspeakably inhospitable four-by-eight cell. Possession and transport of narcotics into Bermuda is, as they say in the fatherland - *verboten*. As they say in Bermuda, 30 years to life.

A shift of the breeze, a gentle cosmic tweak, and I would be rotting in Hell right now. Sometimes, when we think about what might have been, how horrible things have gone for so many around us, we pause - those among us who now and then willingly and mindfully succumb to a graceful pause. We feel, well... lucky. Do I feel like a lucky little punk? Well, do I? Punk?

I am a lucky little punk. Anyway, after having cleared customs for some inexplicable reason, my new wife and I arrived at our honeymoon hotel and lined up with the other cattle of newlyweds. I was struck by how all of the males were rolling their metal bands on their fingers like it was a foreign object newly implanted in our bodies.

We were twisting it, all of us men, and trying to get used to it and telling ourselves we wanted the strange metal band on the third digit of our left hand all along. We, the men and some women - I know now, in particular, my wife - were rethinking our parts in this ridiculous play.

But the show must go on. My wife and I snorted this crappy coke; me, as usual, wanting to fuck on it, but she, as usual, insisted on not. We walked around this island paradise: me, as usual, wanting to drink, and she, as usual, wanting to not. As it turns out, we had nothing to talk about, but we thought that would pass. We thought a nice dinner, a swim in the ocean, or a moped ride would change all that, and we would come out of this no longer feeling like we were playing a part for which both of us had been horribly miscast.

We rode the mopeds; I ingested hundreds of indigenous flies, got brutally sunburned, and, having had some bad Bermuda-style jerked chicken, rode feverishly toward our hotel to violently explode out of my young married ass into a four-star toilet. The weather turned bad almost immediately - a hurricane - and I never got to scuba dive, a dream of mine. But that was the least of my dreams that I didn't realize on this little sobering island of Bermuda.

There was a lover's arch; we walked through it, embarrassed. There was a newlywed's brunch; it tasted wrong somehow - the chef put too much coriander and doubt in it. He was used to cooking for unsophisticated palates, gullets that couldn't distinguish the dubiety. Ours could, and we never went back for seconds.

You know what, though? I recently watched - because for some reason, Clint Eastwood has become a recurring theme here - Escape From Alcatraz, and there is a scene where a beleaguered wife comes to visit her no-good husband, not a real criminal, mind you, just a hard-luck case. She, through the Plexiglas, mouths the words, "I love you, Charlie." She is ravaged; her eyes blood-red, convincingly suffering. Alcatraz was made in 1979, my favorite year, and I realize - my wife would never have given up on me if I had ended up in a prison in Bermuda. She would still be visiting me and mouthing the words, "I love you, Charlie." She would still be there for me; she would always visit me in my prison, wherever that is.

# Home Again Home Again...

I realized I would never feel safe again. There's a feeling when you're married—even when the marriage has stagnated—that on certain days, in certain moments, when you're scared and unsure, you realize you're not alone. There are Sunday nights with Chinese food and a movie. There are moments at the beach, watching your kids build sandcastles while you and your mate steal a glance at each other that says: *You know what? This isn't too bad. We have each other, and we always will.*

These moments are fleeting but powerful. They sustain the marriage, actually—they're nitrous in an empty tank.

Marrieds take them for granted, so busy with resentment that their plates are already full. But when these moments are taken away...

There is no sense of home for us separated, no sense of going home. It's not a structure, not a house, this feeling of security; it's, well, where the heart is. And if the heart is gone, then so goes home. Yes, there is massive love there - my kids, holy shit, my kids - and also with my wife, still and forever, but forever changed. Never again, most probably, will I feel that no matter what, someone has my six. I miss my wingman. It's a bizarre dichotomy: I don't want traditional marriage, but it does, in fact, provide some man-made genome, some crucial chemical that keeps you from withering away in unprotected aloneness. It's flawed, doomed even, but could it be essential somehow for human survival?

I don't know. I just know that it's 50 degrees on August 10th, and I have a fire going. I don't know about Global warming, but I am starting to become an expert on inner cooling. Either way, one can't survive extreme change without adapting.

Happy Anniversary.

Where did everybody go? It's a year ago, to the day, in the Saab.

Where did my wife go? Where did the little microscopic genetic supervisor in charge of the feeling in my arms and legs go?

# August 21.

T he day of the lawn rape, the grabbing of fistfuls of earth, trying to hold on to the planet while my heart and mind spun uncontrollably. The vomiting, the truth. Oh my God.

The truth, the horror, the freedom, the death, the rebirth, the end, but mostly the beginning. The end is really the beginning. Not fun, but nonetheless. But quite frankly, it was a horrible experience; I don't know how many people could survive. I am violently sure I don't know if I will. But I have to try and survive on my own. In fact, is there any other definition of survival other than one's own ability to overcome the hostile elements through individual invention and the primal instinct to live?

To crawl with broken legs in ten feet of snow to where? You don't know. But look, there's a piece of weed to grab onto to pull you forward another inch. That's what life is. To creep, inch by inch, hoping for a remote hunting cabin somewhere beyond the uninhabitable horizon. The night will come soon, and you will die. Do you lie down? You'll die if you do and die if you don't.

Do you want to die trying? I do. I didn't think about how I was living in the context of eventually dying before. But now it's getting dark, and I see a weed, a branch, a rock. And now, living means reaching, grabbing, and pulling me forward for another inch. Inches are life.

Like the inchworm who measures the marigolds, I ask you, does it see how beautiful they are? Are inchworms gender-dependent? Is it a he or a she?

I'm too big to crawl on a marigold, but I know they're pretty amazing, but only recently. Trauma brings clarity. So, I'm rather clear right now.

Either way, Happy anniversary.

# The M.R.I.

I have two Band-Aids on either arm, simply covering the puncture marks. One is from the Lyme disease test, and the other is from the injection of dye prior to my MRI. The Lyme test is uninteresting, a friendly, overweight Russian woman whose life it is to take blood from the young and old, the rich and the not-so-rich - but not poor, not here (it's still a formidable distinction). But we, in the waiting room, looking at each other in stolen glances, are as one: scared as hell, hopeful, and fearful of what this 250-pound woman might discover coursing through our fragile human blood pipes.

The MRI is another matter entirely.

I show up at the hospital and am given a fancy, exciting round pager that beeps and lights up in a circular manner (little LEDs positioned around the edge of the device, the lights going off one after another, like a magical, round runway) when it is my turn.

I am brought back, after I answer the call of the techno-disc, to the chamber.

Now, I am a Star Trek fan - not, in any way, a Star Wars fan. Sorry. I hate tongue-in-cheek; I hate it with a tongueless and cheekless passion. It was an amazing thing, Star Wars, but the fucking little jokes made me wince. I hate winks. They winked in Star Wars; it's the flavor of those films. They wink in the ships, through the battles with the white, plastic Stormtroopers, destroying Death Stars, even as the hero is turned into bronze.

And this device, in this chamber, is straight out of a George Lucas film.

It's bright white; it actually looks like a Stormtrooper's maintenance bay. Where are the red doors to the bridge that opens to Kirk's black leather captain's chair? Not here. This is the revenge of the failed body, episode three. So I lie down on this conveyor, with plugs in my ears and a brace over my head, and am slowly conveyed, like a cyborg in repair, into this chamber - barely big enough to contain my human form. And I can look up, but only that, for you cannot move during this procedure at all - for 30 minutes. I have a strange thought: they had me put my wallet, money, and keys in a locker before and gave me a key to it. But because no metal is allowed, they put the key on the ledge of the window behind which the technicians run the controls. I can't see the key. Where's my key?

Where's the key to my possessions - they're out of my sight? Wait, look up as if I could do otherwise, and there is a little angled mirror like a child's spy periscope, and I can see my feet, the technician's window, and my key.

And then the noises start.

I have earplugs in, but holy shit. They are pulses: loud. The first is a series of laser gun blasts - Blaaaap... Blaaaap... Blaaaap.

Tick-tick-tick-tick-tick-tick-tick.

The various series go anywhere from 30 seconds to 4 minutes at a time. Some of the series have a rhythm, so I started to hum a melody to the enchanting, inhuman, multi-layered sonic blasts. I am in the space station, I imagine, or in some transport going to a hostile planet. I know what I'll find when I egress out of my transport chamber: a race of people who do not understand me or why I'm here. There will be a leader; she will be blonde and beautiful, and I will mate with her.

We will have beautiful cross-species children. And we will both love them, but we will never be able to talk to one another. And one day, she will ask me, "Why did you come here?" And I won't have an answer. Why did I? Was I ever meant to leave my own planet - Planet Me? I was in a strange place; so much of the time, it was hostile, unyielding, barren, and cold. Now I must find a way to get back home, but I can't take my hybrids with me, so I'm fucked. I'll have to stay on this planet but live in a different sector.

I need a tight yellow shirt with black pants tucked into boots.

Oh, and a phaser. No, Mr. Spock, I won't be needing a communicator.

# Too Much Laundry

I got my kids here tonight. My shining jewels of hope and light. I actually named my daughter's middle name Hope. And my son's first name means light. Hope and light. And they are. And I can feel my arms tonight. They are actually giving off heat. Heat! They aren't frozen – it's a miracle, and it's because they're here.

It could also be that I went off my prescribed medications for high cholesterol and high blood pressure. Come to find out, they can make your arms and legs numb. Did my fucking doctor even mention that? Hell no. They don't give a shit about information exchange from people all over the world because there is no money in that.

I read about these drugs – I guess they can save those who refuse to stop eating hamburgers and vehemently oppose moving their rotting carcasses. But I have to believe because I have lost 20 pounds, and perhaps if I can get myself to eat a fucking piece of fruit someday, I can beat this on my own like I have to do with everything else right now.

It could also be related – my tingling limbs – to emotional trauma. But enough with that; I'm sick of washing mucous- and tear-soaked towels.

# The Dirty Snowball

W hat power do we yield to each other? The men to the women, and the women to the men. I can't speak for women. If I could, I wouldn't be here. But I am here, and I like it here now – just now, but certainly not always now. But I can say this about that: I gave up my power, and I need to start to understand why.

You make mistakes, little ones, and they snowball. They – our little wrong path-takers – grow big, enormous, and they lose their purity, whatever purity can exist in the little euphemistic white ball of frozen water.

They become grey, then black with regret. Tainted and filthy. They are unmanageable, tenacious, and shockingly driven. Driven by centrifugal force, which could be equated with life itself: moving, day-changing, motion, time. Driven by "Oh, shit, it's too late now; can't stop the rolling gargantuan, the mistake ball." No – got to roll with it, don'tcha?

This ball – my ball – must be stopped, thawed, and distilled into a palatable energy drink. One that sustains me doesn't destroy me. A delicious lime drink of self-renewal.

Otherwise, I die under the weight of an evil ball of regret that was born to kill. Sidestep, prepare the trap – the hole into which it will fall

– and watch it melt and lose power, giving its power, my power, back to me.

I am eager to watch it scream when it realizes it was duped. I relish the thought of watching it die – melt. GO AWAY.

I will smile at its watery eyes as it – in the disbelieving realization that it is beaten, that I, David, beat this Goliath – will eventually fade away. I will walk away as I can: battered, frost-bitten, and nearly dead. I will smile.

I remember smiling.

# Labor Day

It's Labor Day. My soon-to-be ex-wife is on her way to New York to rehearse with a band she booked that features two terribly famous black stars. Black men freak out for her; she is, after all, the blonde bombshell. They purr and proffer. I have to stop caring. I have to let go. How? Ativan? It works for a while but wears off. I drink; that works, but then it can backfire.

There have been several after-midnight "we should just end this thing" phone calls. I was told to stop the drama, and I suppose I should. So here is the question: How do you turn this machine off? How do I stop caring about her?

I have asked several intelligent friends, some still together, some divorced. "How do you stop feeling like driving off a bridge into a chasm filled with fire and death?"

When I think of my wife with another man, I go even more numb than I already am. I get sweats and chills and am filled with a colorful dread—a solid gas of complete despair and rage. That can't be healthy. So, how do I stop that? I have received the advice of the smartest men I know, and amazingly, they all said the same thing:

"Get a girlfriend."

Ok, I guess that's it then. Problem solved. That shouldn't be too hard to do. Should I go get one right now or after dinner? I'm gonna need one for the holidays; otherwise, it might be lonely. So, I'll get one right before Thanksgiving. Maybe there'd be some kind of run on separated men for fear of being lonely themselves.

The seasons call the times. Last summer, I was dead, and at the end of summer, I was killed. In that death came another life, which lasted through the fall. Then there was winter, and true to its reputation, everything froze again. Only to be burned alive in the spring. Now, it is summer's end again, and it turns out it was the last summer of hope. This last summer, I kept believing in something I now know I have to let go of. What will fall bring? When I look at a leaf changing color right before its fall to loam, will it represent the hope of love lost? Will each leaf's falling be like a mantra:

Let it go...... let it go...... let it go...... let her go.

The tree can do it—why can't I? Could what we had turn orange, fall to the ground, and die, only to make room for something better in the spring? As my wife's mom is wont to say, *"Hope springs eternal."* Either way, this season, this leaf is turning colors and getting ready to fall. I have to let it fall. I have to let her go. I have to let go of the hope hanging around my neck like a skin-chafing albatross.

If one more person says, *"If you love something, set it free... blah blah blah,"* Jesus. Yeah, I know, I have to do it. Maybe I'll take a trip at the end of September and see the morphing foliage. Watch millions of leaves show me how it's done. Watch the ease with which these giant beasts release.

I feel like I have wire snips in my hand. I just don't know which to cut: red, blue, or yellow. It doesn't matter, I know—cut them all.

# I Am Not Ashamed

---

S hould not truth be the child of this unimaginable indignation? To be the "He's separated" guy. To be the "I heard they're getting a divorce" guy. To be the guy, they all want to know who is taking his place. Shame and emasculation. But of what am I ashamed? Who am I answering to? Why should I care what these tennis whites are saying about me?

Here is a poem my friend and brother, Pain Seeker, sent me. It's called "*Do Not Be Ashamed*" by Wendell Berry:

You will be walking some night in the comfortable dark of your yard, and suddenly, a great light will shine around about you, and behind you will be a wall you never saw before. It will be clear to you suddenly that you are about to escape and that you are guilty: you misread the complex instructions, you are not a member, you lost your card, or you never had one. And you will know that they have been there all along, their eyes on your letters and books, their hands in your pockets, their ears wired to your bed. Though you have done nothing shameful, they will want you to be ashamed. They will want you to kneel and weep and say you should have been like them. And once you say you are ashamed, reading the page they hold out to you, then such light as you have made in your history will leave you. They will no longer need to pursue you. You will pursue them, begging for forgiveness. They will not forgive you. There is no power against

165

them. It is only candor that is aloof from them, only an inward clarity, unashamed, that they cannot reach. Be ready. When their light has picked you out, and their questions are asked, say to them: "I am not ashamed." A sure horizon will come around you. The heron will begin his evening flight from the hilltop.

What of that? What of that for me? We all know what of that for all of us. To walk around ashamed, fearing disconnection from the pack. I've always believed that one of the most basic and visceral human fears is the fat boy waiting to be picked for a team in gym.

Fuck them. Let them whisper in hushed tones at cocktail parties. Because someday, they'll be whispering about themselves, to themselves, in a Belvedere-and-Prozac soup, wondering what went wrong and lamenting how sad it is that they couldn't admit they failed to reconfigure the machine that harvests fodder for a lifetime of bickering.

# Senorita Krukowski

My still-estranged wife and I are leveling out now. There will have to be, it seems to me, as the consummate cynic, a time in the future when it explodes. Massive destruction is always on the horizon. Isn't it always? Hasn't it always been? Won't it always be? Why call the wolf out of the forest, though? Leave him be. We are getting along now, letting each other be. I am unsure of not being crippled on a nightly basis; it's downright uncomfortable. I find myself more positive and more compassionate. Bizarre.

I was driving the War Bird through Riverside today with my daughter to get lunch. We were on the main road, the Post Road. I signaled to go left on a less busy but still very busy road whose secret as the "shortcut" has long been compromised. On the corner, waiting for the mechanical signal to tell him to go across this raceway teeming with the finest in Bavarian and German engineering, is a young boy. He is perhaps 12. He sits in a mechanical wheelchair, waiting his turn to motor across the super road. His head is not hanging low like the hopeful little fat boy in the gym; he is not kicking the dirt in mock laissez-faire. He wouldn't be, even if he could use his legs. He does not look beaten at all. How does he do that?

But he does. He does. And I am cowed. The sky is opening. The old me is dead. Fuck him, what an asshole he was. What an ingrate. How can I say this without sounding full of it? I can't. It will. It isn't

167

meant to be. It's just me. I'm just telling you.

Every day, my family, all four of us, can walk to the dinner table, which is a miracle. So much can go wrong. And it does, every minute of every day. It goes wrong. It, and I don't know how, went terribly wrong for that kid in the handicapped scooter, waiting to cross on his own, probably, as I see it, fearless of a mechanical failure; he'd adapt. I haven't even really had to adapt to that degree, and so I am compelled to appreciate what I have for once in my ridiculously one-dimensional life. My little family can walk, and sit and eat and talk and laugh and meld and grow and love and are, every fucking minute of this, the beneficiaries of the beating of the odds. We are the winners, so why shouldn't we act like that? Why haven't I learned to live in grace, humility, and true appreciation for so very long?

What is the benefit of a blind and thankless life?

I don't know, but as my Spanish teacher used to tell me every day because I was always late for class, "*Más vale tarde que nunca.*"[1]

---

[1] Better late than never.

# Good Kind of Asshole

I was visited by a strange and surprising gremlin just now. It hit me out of absolutely nowhere. What if, one day, in the future, she wants me back? I was struck with fear beyond what I can articulate. Sort of the fear when she said she wanted to get married. Where did this come from? Inside this imagined scenario, I find myself creeping backward towards the shadows where I belong. She can't ask for me back, right? Holy shit, but what if she did? I can't handle a relationship! A new wrinkle in this boggling, handmade quilt. I must skulk, slowly, so as not to be noticed, so as not to hurt her again, back to where I belong – which is where?

What kind of an asshole must I be? The good kind, I hope. I hope I'm a good asshole. This is, of course, imagined – this idea that she could love me again. But what of it? Do you know when you realize you're not happy on either side of the fence? What a strange feeling – to not belong on either side, to be sad in the middle, but to feel relieved that for today, you don't have to make a decision that will shackle you for all time. The fence is the place. I can see either side; they both look good, but once I jump, the other side is fenced off to me forever – unless I want to, or she wants to sunder it, rage against it, split it, and jump over its white shards to the other side. Only to find yourself looking longingly over the cracked splinters of your impetuous deed to the side you were just on. No, the fence is better. For now, let me perch.

# In Case I Die

I n case I die, I want you to know I did not make a mistake. I was right.

Beautiful in the beginning, and most beautiful in the end, oh, I know – we're nowhere near the end – but still, your beauty is coming, like an aging Catherine Hepburn. My most high praise, by the way. What a fox.

You are, as it turns out, the most beautiful mother, the most beautiful wife. And the slave who ran back, risking her life to throw me the key. Even though I was your captor.

I lit a fire; it's 84 degrees tonight. But I need the fire – you know what I mean? Despite the temperature, I need the fire. It burns; I burn.

Burning is good.

Do I sound like a pyromaniac? Or could I be in love with fire and anarchy, a man unable to live without madness, without burning alive? You decide; I've already decided. This is me. I like it.

I like this fire on this hot, humid night. I always will now.

And something else: I will always love you from now on.

Boy, it's hot in here! Cold beer bottles sweat water – especially in the heat – it's condensation. Water vapor from air naturally condenses

**OVER ME**

on cold surfaces into liquid water. Water vapor will only condense onto another surface when that surface is cooler than the temperature of the water vapor.

I had to put my laptop down on the same table as my beer. And the water droplets can run like a little river down the surface of my glass top table – down this way or that. So I elevated my laptop: I used a Robert Frost book of collected works to raise my computer above the possible arbitrary runoff of water from my dripping, warming long-neck bottle. Robert Frost is my computer coaster.

I have lit a fire again. But this time, it is raining – not cold, by any means – but sprinkling, nonetheless. The sound of water hitting aluminum gutters in a somewhat predictable pattern, but not really predictable at all, is so wonderfully comforting to me. Yes, the rain is here; I don't know for how long – each sound, each drop is its own – but all of them together is the symphony. And so now, I add fire. I love fire so much.

One is born with a talent, I think. I am extremely talented at loving fire. I remember now because I have the time to remember things, like summers (and winters, sometimes) in Vermont, at my grandparents' house, very near Mount Snow. I remember now, because I have the time, that I would sit and stare at the fire for hours. Transfixed at birth for the burning. No metaphor here; literally, I am in love with fire. I have found her again. Oh yes, I am quite insane.

The light, the heat, the perfect energy of it – it is my obsession. The log, given to the fire, is almost sexual; the fire takes the wood, but not without the wood's permission. My second studio was consumed by fire. I watched all of my master recordings burn. They went first. The room where I stored all I had accomplished in my musical career was closest to where the fire began. Because I had shoveled what I thought were old ashes into a bag and tossed them into the garbage bin behind the studio, they ignited. Goodbye, all my recorded music; goodbye, all my treasured guitars. Shouldn't I hate fire? I love it all

171

the more. It's irrelevant that it ate my life's work; it did no such thing. It enjoyed it like no record company ever did. DATs, cassettes, 2-inch tapes, cable shows, CDs – all of it, gone. So what?

The work is the work; it's not that it can be reproduced. You get me? I just know fire. The birth of man is tied to it. It's fire, rain, the rhythm of ocean waves, crickets and dew and silence, and the maddening, ear-piercing, skittish finch.

The sonic backdrop of waterfalls on this house while the fire rises up to greet it. What else?

Okay, I've lost my mind. But I feel like I've just found it. I wonder, though, if perhaps I should have left it where I found it, just removed the cash.

(Note: I've kept the original content as requested and only made minor adjustments to punctuation, capitalization, and spelling to improve readability.).

# Towers

Today is September 11. That day changed me for a year, and then I went back to the same old shit. We all did, we all have. We should all be different. Why aren't we? People say Americans are bad. But aren't we just people with too much money and time on our hands? If you put all this affluence in Ethiopia, wouldn't they eventually become like us – standing in line for hours, but instead of waiting for water, they are waiting for the new iPhone? Isn't it the human condition rather than the condition of a country? Money is the culprit, greed.

Money had a hand in destroying my marriage, with my assent, of course. Had I really put it as a priority for us, we would still be together and, like everyone else, functioning and relatively happy, I suppose. No one jumping out of either tower six years ago was thinking about money, I bet. The saying is that on your deathbed, no one ever wishes they had spent more time in the office, so then, why do they? Because we – people – say one thing and do another. And the thing we can't stop ourselves from doing is making more and more money. It's a human condition, not an American one.

Columbian warlords do it, Sultan kings, dictators, the loathsome politicians of any country – it's not an American thing; it's a money thing. I know my wife will never get over me not making enough money for this family. I did agree to have two kids, did I not? Aren't

173

I financially responsible for them? Of course I am. Am I not responsible for supporting my wife as well? I should be. Money and power are the aphrodisiacs for women, like a nice ass is for men. So if you don't have some type of power and money, as a man, you ain't gonna get the goods. This makes sense to me, like it or not.

I get stuck on something else here, though: If you do it all correctly, you follow the rules, you don't get happiness either. The couple ages and grows apart – it's inevitable following the pattern of traditional marriage; the woman goes through the "change," the man is hornier than ever, and the marriage sours like expired milk.

The man retires, the woman can't believe how much he's home now, and the couple, once fresh-faced and hopeful, standing on the church steps in a tux and white dress, with the sun shining in her golden hair, is now sitting in different corners of the TV room, watching bad commercials over and over again. Not talking. When the talking starts, you wish it didn't.

Kids are behind you, death is in front, and nothing but contemptuous prattle exists as you wait. Can it be otherwise? I certainly hope so. My wife and I are entering a period where there is much less drama – no poignant emails, no teary drop-bys, no late-night phone calls – in other words, we're settling down. Yes, we have removed the bickering, the bile of contempt, the murderous familiarity, but are we adding anything good? Or should I believe that taking the bad away is good intrinsically? It doesn't feel good intrinsically.

The marriage we had before was a marriage without drama, without sex, without intimacy. What's different now, except the removal of negativity? I feel like we're drifting apart again, only this time it's for keeps.

She talks of going to our Florida house for Thanksgiving. "Where am I going to sleep?" I ask. "Can't we sleep in the same bed?"

"Ummmm," she hesitates.

Does she mean to insinuate that we could possibly make love? I don't ask; I know better by now – she doesn't know – but imagine getting rejected in Florida. No, thank you.

Florida has a feeling of being trapped anyway. Imagine the long walk to cool off in the warm, humid Florida air. Actually, by Thanksgiving, that doesn't sound too bad. But it would set me back to be rejected again. And worse, if she initiated it, and I didn't perform well – gee, I wonder what the odds of that happening are – I would feel even worse. I'm trapped for the time being.

We've got to protect ourselves in the end, don't we? We turn on each other. We hurt in ways unimaginable to strangers, the very people we swore to protect and cherish. It's a beautiful life, but it's really hard if you actually live it.

It's not an American thing; it's a human thing.

Happy 9/11.

# The Catsup in the Wry

M y friend and I lit a fire at her house. The art of fire is such that if you build it in a pyramid-like shape, in other words, small logs forming a teepee, to begin with, then add bigger ones once the pyre has taken hold, you will have a successful fire every time. Our teepee was in full triangular success mode, the fire burning beautifully, and then she did it.

I had suggested, at the beginning of building the fire, that we hadn't enough kindling, and I, funny as I am, suggested that because we hadn't enough proper kindling, maybe we should use a book. She said, without missing a step, as it were, "I have an extra copy of *Catcher in the Rye*."

"Burn J.D. Salinger? Are you insane?"

"Fuck it, it's an extra copy."

"What are we, Germany?"

"No," she said, "We just need more kindling."

The fire went on without needing to burn the master, so we didn't.

Then, in an idle moment, I picked up _The Catcher in the Rye_ and read various random selections. How can this be? I thought, this really isn't very good at all, and I was shocked. I must be wrong. I absolutely have to be wrong.

I said to her, "This sucks, but it can't, it's *The Catcher in the Rye*."

I continued to search for something to prove me to be the ignoramus that I am. I began to read aloud a promising passage, but it broke that promise. Passage after passage.

Simone, moving like a ninja, lunged at me and, in one motion, grabbed *The Catcher in the Rye*, snatched the required reading from my hands, and flung it into the fire. It landed atop the pyramid of logs. It became a burning skull and crossbones. We had inadvertently created the perfect Jolly Roger.

The book burned beautifully, with purpose, actually, like it was meeting its fate.

Then, the burning head appeared to wink at me, a red, glowing, blinking eye, like a pirate eye! It looked first like a grasshopper, but then a praying mantis, but always a maniacal face atop the crossbones.

Oh, Mister Salinger, I have to believe this would make you laugh. Can I be arrested for this?

# Balsamic Vin-Regret

These are the brisk days of September. I love them – sunshine, dry and cool. Here in Chickahominy, in the severance shelter, my little backyard has exploded with birdsong. I don't know what's caused the ruckus. I asked them – the finches, the cardinals, the red-breasted robins, and whoever else – what's happened? Why the fuss? Did I do something? I'm just sitting outside in the sun, eating my Al Pacino – sweet soppressata, mozzarella, roasted pepper with lettuce and tomato on a roll from Bella Cucina. I know I'm bothering the bee because he wants in on my sandwich. (It must be the balsamic vinegar driving him wild; I leave him a puddle on the table). But the birds, why the cacophony? Is it the radio? I turn off the radio, but they continue to warble and chirp. Is it that they sense fall coming, that they're panicked about the ensuing cold? I will never know, but I love their passion.

I am a smidge hungover – as I had met my friend and his girlfriend for drinks at a bar in Greenwich called MacDougall's. It was four o'clock in the afternoon. My friend's wife was in New York, seeing a Broadway play. So he had some time. This is what is happening all around me, and it's becoming normal – unhappy housewives, cheating husbands, remarriages, and shuttling kids between first and second sets of parents. As for me and my lovely wife, there is little movement as we head into the sixth month of me living out of the house. She has booked the family to go to our house in Lighthouse Point, Florida, for Thanksgiving, so apparently, I'm going. She has requested that my parents and I not talk about the separation during this holiday. She wants a vacation from it – a vacation from what? We haven't talked about what's going on for months. The silence between us has become the norm, S.O.P. I don't say anything because, well, that's what we're doing now. So, I look forward to continuing to discuss the breakdown and consequent breakup of our marriage in the sunny, humid Florida air. Heat the pool, put the turkey in the oven, and bring on the silence! I look forward to a feast of quiet denial.

# The Hissing

L ife is not mine. What I have is something else. I have fantasy, film, hope, and books about hope, tragedy, and works of beautiful fiction – living in an artistically created world. I think I just can't exist here.

The real world assaults my senses like a factionary, ill-informed military invasion. This can't be. This is not happening – they aren't shooting me and those I love, are they? The "they." I don't like the "they." The good can't protect themselves; they're too busy trying to dream. I will die with them – the dreamers and hopers – as I should, every minute loving my perfect children, the origin of dreams.

To survive requires a steadfast hardiness, which I do not possess. I am weak but strong in heart, which can't possibly defend itself. I'm a bird with a broken wing, hissing at the approaching bringer of death – the cat, the ants, the larvae. I will hiss the whole time; the sound will be all that remains – my final, feeble defense.

# Side Effects

It's fascinating to contemplate the idea that we, to a certain extent, shape our own realities. Our thoughts, actions, and choices, even the unconscious ones, can influence the course of our lives. It's as if we're the architects of our own destiny, laying brick by brick, sometimes consciously, often unconsciously.

Your journey is a testament to this. You've navigated through challenges, made choices, and ultimately found yourself in a place of peace and solitude. It's a powerful realization that we have the ability to reshape our lives, even when it feels impossible.

The concept of being alone, yet not truly alone, is a profound one. We often seek companionship to fill voids, but true fulfillment often comes from within. It's a journey of self-discovery, of understanding our own desires and needs.

As you've mentioned, the past is a complex tapestry of choices and consequences. It's important to acknowledge the role we played in shaping our circumstances without dwelling on regrets. Instead, we can focus on the present moment, embracing the freedom and solitude we've cultivated.

It's inspiring to see your newfound appreciation for the simple things in life. The comfort of your own space, the freedom to dress as you please, and the quiet moments of reflection are all valuable treasures.

As you continue on this path of self-discovery, remember to be kind to yourself. Embrace the journey, the good and the bad, and trust in your ability to shape your own reality.

Sit silently in the grass for an hour and ask yourself: Who do I want to be, and where do I want to be doing that? Sit silently every day and make sure you are right lest you feel responsible for taking up 20 years of someone else's life. Not to mention your own.

Listen. You are speaking. Your voice is strong inside you. Obvious when you crack the code. The code is things. Noise. Bullshit. Crack it. Wide open. And from the cracks in the shell of the code will first be silence, then a breathing sound of the universe sighing with relief, and then, faint at first, your voice, and you cock your head, point your ear like repositioning rabbit ears on an old TV set for better reception, but you won't have to, because as long as you are silent, the voice will get louder, clearer, stronger, and its message will be unmistakable. It will bring despair and then joy. Live them both; they are branches from the same tree, they are words of the same voice, they bring you back to you, and suddenly you stop lying, pretending, accepting what does not fit.

Ill-fitting things. The voice from the silence burns out the bullshit like broiling Sun rays clearing the fog. It just happens automatically. I must walk around now and shake my limbs so that I can better feel them.

Oh, did I forget to mention? There may be some side effects.

# Marriage

---

"Marriage"

By Wendell Berry

How hard it is for me, who lives in the excitement of women and has the desire for them in my mouth like salt. Yet you have taken me and quieted me that other women have been your shadows.

You come near me with the nearness of sleep. And yet, I am not quiet. It is to be broken. It is to be torn open. It is not to be reached and come to rest in ever. I turn against you. We hurt and are hurt and have each other for healing. It is healing; it is never whole.

Isn't it obvious? Marriage isn't the answer. It's the question. Commitment, by its nature, breeds white lies, and by its nature, by not wanting to hurt the other because you said you love each other forever, you cannot do otherwise but candy-coat. Every doubt is subverted, and every desire for another is put away in a place that never goes away and comes back to haunt you like an indolent and precocious ghost.

Regret is a tsunami. It's just a matter of time.

I am going to an open house tonight for my children at their school. I will be going with my wife, who I am starting to see more

183

and more as the Helena character in *"Boxing Helena."* She is screaming at me because she can't move, and I am apparently the one who cut off her arms and legs.

Once you see that they are damaged, in fact, in many ways unable to even walk, in a metaphorical sense, they take on a different role in your life. The power is waning. What she thinks of me is slowly starting to matter less. Things are done by the married sometimes out of fear of what the other might think or do.

Think about the beginning of a relationship. Obviously, because you both want to have sex, you want the other to like you, but if they don't like something fundamental about you, you question the likelihood of a permanent connection. You might overlook it, or you might move on. But you're not *afraid* of them.

My wife wants to have drinks with me before attending this event.

This event, the parents of their children sitting in tiny seats (their kid's seats and desks) and listening to the "curriculum" of the school, is a trial to endure. We are attending both the kindergarten and fourth-grade presentations. I would rather jump in a pile of horse shit. Wait, that's just what I'll be doing. I have to sit with all these yuppie puppets in the stifling air, blinded by fluorescent lights, listening to their polyester business suits swishing as they readjust their large hedge fund bodies in these tiny little chairs in which their innocent spawn try to soak up the world according to the American Board of Education.

I like the teachers; they are doing good work. Teaching is a service that is terribly undervalued and underpaid. I am getting intimate with that fact now that I'm teaching.

I went to the "open house," loitering outside the auditorium (the very same one where I performed a stunning rendition of H.M.S. Pinafore's "The Admiral of the Sea") as the Wall Street Bulls and Cows sat and watched a "PowerPoint presentation." The herd was treated to a series of images of poor children who didn't get a proper education. Huh, what could they possibly be looking for? The images were accompanied by sad classical music bristling out of an antiquated public address system; it was spitting and cackling, going in and out. I'll donate some money for a new PA system! But I didn't really see much; I was walking outside, talking to trees and smelling the dewing grass.

After the presentation, we were herded to our children's classroom, where the teacher informed the parents that my son had told the class that his father had complained about these things being so boring. I took my bow and took my seat in the back near the window, struggling to get a whiff of the outside.

The stick figures asked inane questions, and it was mercifully over. Another important night for our society. Afterward, our Bingo friends asked us for a drink at the local marble and wainscoting drinking establishment. There are plasma TVs over the urinals.

We went; my wife didn't have a drink, she doesn't really like it, and I downed two martinis. I dropped my wife off at my father's house and left the stifling and high-energy atmosphere of Old Greenwich, heading back to a simpler place where peeling Caucasian lawn jockeys hold up broken lamps.

Children are born from perfunctory sex. Ours were. The women tell the men that they're ovulating, and the men acquiesce. It's a woman, for God's sake, wanting sex. Does it matter that she really doesn't want it? Not to us!

There is a woman wanting sex.

I remember it now, the requisite blowjob, the illusion of passionate interest, all geared to get pregnant. This isn't a complaint; it's how it is. Women, when they decide to get pregnant, become Paul Revere, running through the town shouting, "I'm ovulating, the baby is coming, the baby is coming!"

And we, the townspeople, react and run up to the bedroom, flaccid and confused, and give them what they want, and what we want, but for excruciatingly different reasons. And so, life comes from this, but it's not bad. It's just confounding and interesting in the most profound way.

I came in a cup at New York Hospital. I ran and answered the call of the ovulating woman, and we conquered, despite passion, and we created two miracles despite the absence of what should probably have been a magical and natural experience. But it isn't.

I am burdened, like a swayback pack mule, with the absence of you. No calls, no emails, no nothing. You used to call me for no reason; it was endearing. You used to email me with your sadness; it gave us a connection. You stopped by once, for no reason, in the morning; it was inspiring. Now, there is nothing, and it is barren and broken.

Your disconnection from me is like jumping into ice water. It's shocking. This is what you want. And because you have asked this of me, I give it to you: Nothing. And you call me not and write me not and show up at my door not.

OK. I will give my drama to only me now, to my broken, freezing body, fast becoming intolerable, but it's the only vessel built to withstand the force. I'm a bomb squad blowbox. I made the bomb; I am the bomb. I'll absorb the force of the explosion. Why not?

I miss you, though. I sure miss you, my little shard-absorbing bomb blanket. Rainer Maria Rilke says solitude is sacred. Maybe it is, but it's a fucking hard road. It's a road that draws a few, a straggling band that has no other way to go, a road that is compelling to only two or three or four. It's a suicide road, a road we could not possibly have chosen. This road chose us.

Dramatic? You think so? Fuck you. How do you like them apples? But maybe you don't judge me so harshly, so, not fuck you, but thank you.

# Climbing

M y humor is gone from me. I have to believe that it will return. It feels like it's been distilled and steamed out of the pot. What is left is cold and brittle, and yet stronger than before, but sadder, certainly. My laughter has always been my salve on this rope burn of an existence. I guess, as I tend to my burning hands (freezing actually, the same, really), I need to pause to look up or down to see if my palms are chaffed from sliding down or climbing up. Shouldn't I know what direction I'm going? If I have to endure what at times feels unendurable, then I think I'm entitled to know where I'm headed, then continue on or change course entirely. From what I can tell, I think I'm headed up. It's harder, for sure, but if I give in to exhaustion, the plunge downward would light my hands afire and burn off the flesh to the bones. And then, when I finally hit the ground, I would have bone hands. Funny little Halloween hands. Sharp, whitish, smoking skeleton prongs that could no longer feel anything. And then I couldn't hold a pen, stroke nylon strings, or hold your face.

Funny, as I decide to pull up another millimeter, grunting with pain, fear, and sureness, I am climbing farther away from your face. Climb! Climb!

# The Big Brown Monster

I have my children in Old Greenwich for the weekend. Being here is a blessing and a curse, healing and sickness. It's a museum where my life used to be, perfectly preserved. Every stick of furniture is where it was back in that era. It looks just like it did when they lived here: husband and wife, two children, and a cat.

When I come here now, I'm a landscaper, a cleaning lady, and I wander through it like a displaced, politically incorrect American. To lie in the bed, perfectly preserved, it looks just like it did back in the old days, is nothing short of unreal. Looking at the ceiling is like me looking through my own eyes back in time. What was I thinking about letting that marriage go on as it was for so long? Is it a coincidence that they call it lying in bed? You made your bed. Now lie in it.

The oddest thing about being here is I have no idea what to do with myself. There's nothing for me here now. Does the snake ever visit its shed skin? Does the crab go back and hang out in its abandoned shell?

There are sounds coming from the ever-encroaching neighbors, whose children bring noise as they grow. There is an adopted boy next door who seems to think he is going to be a major league pitcher; the ball never stops smashing into the tired old wood of the fence. Each time an errant fastball careens into it, it creaks, pulls ever so slightly off its mooring nails, and softens and splinters. There will come a day when the mighty Cambodian will literally bring down the fence. The big brown monster.

Then there are the countless barking dogs, abandoned for hours at a time by their human hosts, constantly woofing at the universe in maddeningly unpredictable patterns. With all these noises, old neighbors, old blue stones, and old ponds, you have lost your charm today. I need to buy a frame that holds two pictures in it, side by side or one on top of another. One picture will hold the memories of my childhood here; the other will be a snapshot of the memories of my adulthood here. One was happy, the other not so much. Then I need to put this picture away. I need an attic. This house doesn't have one, and neither does View Street. It doesn't matter because this isn't literal anyway. I need to put all this behind me. I need to go forward. Why does that make us sad to move on? Why do we feel we need to stay? Stay where? Why?

Millions of people have come before me and had to walk away from the only life they could remember living. What I'm going through is not new, and there must be lots of great advice out there about how to safely navigate this thistle-laden path. I don't know why I don't want to hear about it, why I don't want to really walk through the soul-slashing branches to get to the other side, tend to my wounds, and walk forward, leaving it behind me forever. It feels safer somehow to just crouch here, in a little dirt clearing I have discovered, free of the lancing thorns that await me if I move. If I brace myself, wince, and move forward fast enough, don't you see it will be truly over?

Over.

I'm just not ready for that. I'm going to have to eat something soon, though; I've picked this poison berry bush clean.

# Mourning Wood

I bought wood for my fire tonight from a huge ShopRite superstore. They spelled Rite Wrong. The wood came in a little, ready-to-carry, shrink-wrapped pack with a little rope handle stapled to the top. It must have come from somewhere in a nearby forest or one not nearby; I can't know. But after I placed it into my fireplace and after it gave me heat, I smelled my hands as I rubbed my face in emotional exhaustion. And my hands smelled like that forest that lay nearby or far away.

I thought this was what intelligence smelled like. They are smart, these trees. They're OK with pounding rain or searing sun. They like mold or clearings. They're good like that. They cover or relent to better coverers. They grow if we let them, for hundreds of years, and if we don't, they give us shelter as timber or heat as logs, but always they give. They are actually responsible for much of our breathable oxygen; they also breathe in our poisonous exaltations. They give us shade, or if we cut them down, they give us life as warmth we might soon have no alternative to.

Tree hugger? Oh yes. I hug them. I sit under them, I swoon from their smell, and I burn pieces of them, but first, I give them their due. But mostly, I realize how off we are, how much we are not like them, how we don't live in harmony, how we take and take and take but only give if there is an angle of getting thereof. Tonight's laptop coaster is

190

Yeats.

Tonight, I love my wife. Tonight, like any other night, I am comforted by the forest, by the simple truth of the rising giants. We can't compete with them, though we try every minute of every day. But when humans' time is done, they will, as they do, pick up the pieces and grow.

Can't see the forest for the trees? The forest IS the trees. Marriage plus time equals an unwanted, unperceived numbing. I have stepped back and looked upon it; I am learning to smell. The days shouldn't be numbered but tasted. Years should not fly by at all, but be slow. We should taste life, and roll it around in our mouths, before swallowing, rather than sucking it down like a Big Gulp at Seven Eleven.

I had a good day with my wife and family because I WAS THERE. What a nice place my family is. What a wonderful smell it leaves on my heart. I can't wait to see them again tomorrow unless I'm cut down by the big lumberjack in the sky. But if I'm not, I can't wait to shelter them, or fall for them, or show them how to grow by the bylaws of the giants, who be bark or human brilliance. Who is Redwoods or Einsteins? But both cut from the same cloth… grateful and listening, growing and open to life itself.

I'm going to go get another bundle of wood. It's like a teeny piece of the universe at only $5 a pop.

191

# No More Free Frosty's

I have just learned that my next-door neighbor here in Chickahominy is a Vietnam vet who has a propensity for beating people with a baseball bat. He also has a loaded gun in his apartment. Oh, happy day.

So it turns out this little "safe house" is sitting among the demons. The truth is, of course, they're everywhere. I just found out about one of them right in my backyard. Of course, I found this out from my other neighbor, who has just switched from working at Wendy's to McDonald's, so no more free Frosties for me.

And as she wove her story about the vet, she also told me her kids, who live with her above the vet, broke into his apartment and stole his drugs, of which there are plenty, apparently. So, I am living among thieves, thugs, and incompetent mothers.

JUST LIKE OLD GREENWICH!

# F Holes

I knew what I was and what I was good at an early age. And then I forgot. So, who's to blame?

I love her so much, and she'll never know because I'm such an asshole.

I burned a guitar tonight; it was a piece of shit, but it was a guitar nonetheless. I'm a terrible mess.

I want to talk to my mother. But she's in Florida.

I want to hold my wife, but she's asleep in another house entirely - not wanting to hold me back.

I want her to know how much I love her, but I've bungled that in a most competent and efficient manner.

I want her again, or maybe for the first time, but the window has closed, it seems, and it can't reopen. She seems to have rigged it shut.

I see her now through the closed window - is it one-way glass?

She can't see me, but she could for so long, and I squandered it for longer. I lost it because my selfishness won over her love.

And so, fuck me.

It feels about right. I am too little, too late.

Boy, the lacquer fumes are taking their toll. Or are the burning, glowing F-holes trying to tell me to wake up and honor more than her, but honor me and my love for her?

I don't know; I just know that we die, and I need to hurry up and appreciate love before it fades away, as it might have with my wife - but maybe not, so try, so try, so try.

In case it's still there.

I will try to show her my love until I'm told to stop. Oh, the wisdom of burning F-holes.

# Deposit

I went to cash some checks today from teaching; unfortunately, I use Bank of America, which should consider renaming itself Bank of *Amigo*. In their slew of massive standalone advertisements for opening checking accounts, refinancing mortgages, or getting $25 for recommending a friend, I could not see a word written in English. *Mama mia.*

On my way into the "bank," I noticed there was smoke coming from beneath a small tree. I walked away from it at first, thinking it might be an incendiary device. Then I shook off my new millennium chicken-shit mentality and walked up to it to investigate. After all, I'm in Byram, not Fallujah. The mulch around the small tree had ignited from some gentleman's cigarette. Because, as we all know, the world is their ashtray! I had to stomp this mini-blaze out with my sandals purchased at Target for $17.99. It took a few minutes, and several people stared at the crazy white man stomping on the base of a tree, muttering to himself, "Jesus Christ, what is it with me and fire? *¡Ola!*"

The smoke and fire are calling me every day. Is it telling me to burn my bridges? To burn the evidence of the old me, of my old life? Or to burn the haze off on the shore to reveal the truth? Or am I looking too hard at life and its meaning? Should I just go about my business like everyone else and stop trying to see things so deeply? Alas, I cannot. This last part of my life, the final 1/3, the last 30%, should be spent in awareness, I think. If my body can stand it, that is. My arms and legs burn now from the tingling sensation, worse in the morning, perhaps because I now dream about my problems with my wife, only to wake up to them in the morning.

The good news, however, is that I got my *dinero*, and tonight, I'm going to spend some of it on a good amount of Corona Light. *¡Buena suerte!*

# Numbness and Neighbors

I don't feel particularly well these days. My limbs don't just tingle. They pound with pain. No one knows what the fuck is wrong, but I think I do; my mind said fuck you to my body, and my body said no, fuck YOU.

I've got one neighbor on one side skulking in the dark, waiting to bash my head in with a baseball bat because he thinks I think he's gay, and another neighbor on the other side revving his suped-up Toyota Celica in front of my house because he thinks I call the cops and have them remove the various unregistered vehicles he regularly tows home for what purpose I could never fathom. But one night, while he sat in his "noise makes the dick seem bigger" mobile with his small "engine" sounding "big" from the modified muffler configuration, I came out, stood on my front stoop, and yelled at him to turn the fucking car off already; he thinks that I call the cops to remove his revolving collection of future noise-making tin junk on a basis as regular as he tows them in. I have not called even once, but I don't deny, either, that I have reveled when I see the cruiser and the tow truck, my dynamic duo tirelessly fighting the evil obsessive Las Automan! Collector of rusting crap! Installer of cheap noise-making muffler enhancers! Blaster of shitty music!

It is so loud that the very air around this small fossil fuel-burning combustion engine-driven conveyer of a useless life undulates and sets tree branches quivering, sending little winged animals flying away in shock and self-defensive disbelief. But he underestimates the power of the good and the quiet... he underestimates the commitment of the protectors of sanity... Cruiser and Tow! Keepers of the quiet and enemy of the space takers! Sworn to protect this world from unregistered heaps of useless shells of metal and stinking, drinking guzzlers—dioxide crapulous noise makers, assaulters of the air we breathe and the sound we need to hear; not them, the vehicles of the damned.

Who will come out victorious?

# The Meaning of Fingers

Television commercials are so confusing to me. The Mercury girl is intoxicating and breathtaking; then, in the blink of an eye, it's the Lubriderm girl whom I would gladly die for. As men, we are just terribly torn, to our core, about physical beauty. I'm not making the played-out argument that we are what we are because of what is pushed upon us every minute of every day – in subway ads, commercials, movies, music videos, books, magazines, newspaper ads, posters of physical perfection on walls, windows, the plethora of magical beauties in Times Square, the billboards, the internet, and the every God-forsaken product; from cars to apple orchards. I'm not saying we, as men, are not responsible for our behavior, but still.

Women are pursuing more and more the modern-day equivalent of the water sipped from the Holy Grail: physical immortality, vis-à-vis a staggering statistical rise in plastic surgery.

Tonight, my laptop coaster is William Carlos Williams. I wonder about something: Why does every digit have a name, but not the one that is numb to me? We have the thumb, the index finger, the middle finger, and the pinky. Now, what about that other one? The ring finger? We define this finger, which I can no longer feel, as an accouterment – an accessory? This is the finger that can only be described on one hand, so no, it's not good enough. My right hand has that finger and no ring. Neither does my left hand anymore, so no deal

199

– not the ring finger. I propose that finger shall now be called the finger I can no longer feel – the lost finger, the ringless finger. Mine is a ringless, touchless digit.

It can't be a coincidence – I don't believe in them. I am starting not to believe in anything except myself. And what am I but a broken puzzle? Put my dead finger on the board now and start to piece this thing together. Use my ringless digit to let its shaky, purposeful movement guide this cardboardian representation of fleshy life to make itself clear. Let my weakness show me my strength. Maybe it will stop shaking and become un-numb once I let it do its job. You got any better ideas?

# The Anniversary

---

Tomorrow is your 17-year wedding anniversary. You've decided on no gifts, not even cards because your wife hates writing. Her words are a sad indicator of her inability to verbally communicate her deepest feelings. Funny, her father was an intellectual, read everything, and knew just about everything, except he must have missed the book about not driving into a gully. Or maybe, actually, he DID research a fast, easy way out of this tawdry existence, a way out of his miserable life with his miserable, drunken wife.

Are you looking for your ditch? Not literally, of course. Your children are far too young to suffer without you. When they get older and start suffering with you, you'll rethink. But for now, how do you escape the cage you built? And what of tomorrow, with your plans for a nice dinner? What do two separated people talk about on their wedding anniversary? In a word, nothing.

It's what you do now. You don't communicate. IT'S LIKE YOU'RE MARRIED. You thought you were supposed to be closer to all this stripping of resentment and familiarity. You don't hate each other, but you're definitely estranged. She will, you expect, start the evening with the pre-requisite: "Tonight, I just want to have fun; I don't want to talk about anything heavy."

"OK... so... what's... how's... WAITER, I'M GONNA NEED ANOTHER DRINK, PLEASE."But tomorrow isn't today, and for today, you're bringing your son back here for the night. This means South Park, meatball wedges with Doritos crumpled on them, PlayStation, hitting each other with the Junk Ball (essentially a whiffle ball designed to make a strange sound as you wing it as hard as you can at your opponent, the one who leaves the reddest welt on the other wins, thank you, Jackass), staying up late, hacking around, and enjoying each other in a most basic and wonderfully primitive way. You can't wait.

# Maximum

T here is a silent partner for me here. He is black and angry and abandoned.

He wonders why I'm not there every night to snuggle. And mostly every morning. He can't rationalize this tweaking of the status quo. He - every day I come by - is yowling in his way; his disbelief of my disappearance, his justified cries of "Where the fuck did you go? I've been with you for 16 years. What the fuck happened?"

I wish I could answer him better, but I shush him away amidst his annoying meows because his questions resonate too profoundly, don't they? Max is right to scream at me at the top of his elderly lungs. He's been with me from the beginning, and I'm with him. Yes, he's just a cat, but he's more than that to me - he's my partner. And he's pissed and confused.

Max, and someday my son and my daughter, I have no simple explanation as to what caused the catastrophic change in our lives. Max is not happy. He lost his snuggle partner. Where my wife, oddly, doesn't miss that at all because she never liked to snuggle. She is, at the end of the day, quite cold. But at the beginning and middle of the day, shockingly warm and selfless.

Oh, Max, my consort, my cohort, my feline soul mate, I have chosen to sacrifice you. Forgive me. I know you can.

Black fur, tattered ears, and angry caterwauling - I am you, only fleshy and spotted. I, too, am pissed and confused, and shaking my head wildly from side to side, like a cartoon with its *wada wada wada* sound effects, wondering: What the fuck happened?

Wada wada wada. Wada wada wada.

# Seventeen

Our 17-year anniversary came and went. I took her to Ruby's Oyster House in Rye, New York. I had some nice steamers in a feted concoction of a vile weed called leek with some broth. My wife had a disgusting seafood mess on toasted yet soggy bread. She had wine, and I had two shots of vodka and several beers. There was a nice iceberg slice with some frigging Roquefort dressing. $85.00 for a fucking piece of lettuce and a whiff and smack of low tide.

We talked about our favorite new subject: other people's miserable marriages. She has a friend who is having an affair, as do I, so we have so much in common, don't we? It was a nice time. On the way home, I broached the subject again. It's what I do.

I talked about the fact that since everything is different between us, which it is, doesn't it stand to reason that the sex would be better, or at least different? I hit the wall that I have come to know as her face – stony, impassive. She cried for a second but wasn't able to say why. That's helpful. She just repeated her mantra – that it's all about chemistry, and we never really had it. When will I give this campaign up? When will I make the call and concede?

We came back to what I must now call my place and watched a terribly mediocre Albert Brooks movie, "Looking for Comedy in the Muslim World." I think he had better refine his search – or broaden it.

We sat on the couch together, her body language a harsh warning of standoffishness. She looked beautiful, but what of it? So I sat and watched and suffered in silence. Nothing wrong with suffering in silence – I've come to find out that it empowers you. It gives the suffering meaning if it's yours alone. And so I am gaining power through suffering.

Oddly, the day after, she was terribly nice. She seemed quite content with this configuration. She still had me as her children's father; I still mowed the lawn, and I still cleaned the house when I was there. Please, someone, tell me why. I still sat and talked to her; she loved to talk to me. She just didn't know how hard it was for me to sit there and not drag her upstairs – and, you know. We still did family events and such, so she had the best of everything right now. She was going out a lot, doing a lot of things, and she was feeling good about herself. Good stuff, right?

Well, she had gone too far.

She had booked us to go to our Florida house for Thanksgiving. What was I thinking? I agreed to this, but now I realized I found it unacceptable that I was once again relegated to sleep elsewhere than the master bed. It was for the master, wasn't it? So I told her to cancel that – right out. She acted shocked and bewildered; she looked at me like I had wounded her. Oh, poor thing. You don't get to go on a vacation and pretend that everything's all right. We'd be playing house – it would be spectacularly sad. And at the end of every night, I would go stay at a friend's house or sleep with my parents in their hotel room. The idea of living in the same house with her, all the while her not even once glancing in my direction, made me ill. It triggered something in me – or maybe it was our anniversary, which I guess I had hoped for something more than nothing. But I felt kicked back to the beginning; I felt bashed. I was looking one way and turned around for just a second – only to see, at the last second, the grill of a truck. I've got the letters "KCAM" (backward) stamped on my forehead. The force of the collision knocked me back to when I first realized she didn't want me anymore. I guess I thought that would change. It hasn't. It's worse than the beginning because it's fast becoming real. I have to start thinking about this now. I have to start thinking like a divorced man – that's different than a separated man. Much, much different.

# More

---

ook how I default, like a trained seal, to my side of the bed. I am in Old Greenwich, in our old bed, her current bed, I guess, but it's like visiting for me. It's fucking late. She's in New York, seeing "*Young Frankenstein*," the musical; she coordinates the cast album recordings. Very glamorous. I bet it sucks. She's going to go back to View Street after the show, so I'm here in my past.

I roll over to the right, my old side, and marvel at how small this bed is, especially in comparison to my king-size monstrosity in Chickahominy, to hold two full-grown adults who hardly ever breached the line in the middle to touch each other. How small the bed, how massive the space between us – we were right there, barely an inch between us, and we didn't touch. How did this happen, on a level, going on the better part of two decades? I smell her here, but she's gone. I never smelled her when she was here before. She was right here all along, and so was I, such as I am, but we erected a Plexiglas wall between us in the middle of this bed every night – night after night, year after year.

Why?

How?

Why?

Oh God, why?

Good night, my ghost.

# Get a Girlfriend

---

I walk around these days trying to ignore the fact my legs are permanently dipped in ice water. As time goes on, I find, interestingly, that the pain doesn't lessen, but our connection does. We are going our separate ways without admitting it. We are telling ourchildren by the way we live that we are no longer a family but rather a life scheduled around pick-ups and snuggles and sleepovers. The fact she wants me to date and, in fact, have sex with other women is not something I can get used to, but, and so, I am going to do it. The thought of her doing it turns my guts into a sick, dark swamp, and so I force myself not to think about it too much. But it's hard to choose what to think about. This particular thought chooses me several times a day, accompanied by the thought that she no longer wants to be intimate with me, or, as she says, she just doesn't know yet.

I have an appointment with a shrink on Friday and, immediately after, a date with a redhead.I hope the shrink will tell me how to deal with this madness, and I hope the redhead will deal madly with me.

So they were right.Go get a girlfriend.Imagine that.

My father sent me a box of books about how to make a marriage work. I suppose he hasn't been listening. She doesn't want it to work. She just doesn't want to admit that yet.The truth is that this is the chickenshit approach, as opposed to the Band-Aid ripping. Approach. And while I'm at it, do *I* want it to work? If I actually ask myself that question, my blood pressure will rise like a shifting ocean shelf. When the two giant tectonic plates rise and swell, they create a tidal wave. When my blood pressure rises to 155 over 108 like it did yesterday, that's almost dead. But I have to ask myself this question:

Do I really want her back?

Let me ask another question so as to quickly divert my attention. If you asked a long-time married man if he *could,* without any complications at all, go out and have sex with other women and sleep in his own house whenever he wanted to but not lose the money or the children, what might he say? If you asked a long-time married man or woman if they still desperately wanted their spouses, what would they say? Do men and women

*really* want to spend day after day after day with each other, I mean, if they *could* choose? Everyone I talk to about having my own little house moans with envy. They coo. I watch their eyes glaze over like they are looking into one of those computer-generated posters that reveal a 3D image of a spaceship within a seemingly nonsensical configuration of colored dots and smears. It's not fun here sometimes, but it *breathes*. The air is not heavy with the specter of a limited future. Things don't seem finished here but have begun. There is not a sense of things closed but rather a sense of openness, like a freshly popped strawberry preserves jar with its sucking sound as the wax seal gives way. Yes, there is a price: my body. The trauma has taken its toll. Yes, there is the question of how long

before the jam starts to mold, how long it will last, or whether I have enough toast to enjoy this sweet, succulent nectar.

I just think I would rather fill my house with its tart essence for as long as I can rather than climb *into* a jar, hold my breath and screw the lid tightly closed.

Bon Appetit.

210

# Ramping Down

It has been months since I have written a word. Christmas looms in the grey winter landscape, and a blanket of snow has come to quiet the Northeast part of planet Earth. But it seems to be coinciding with a quieting that has taken place somewhere even closer. The snow cover seems to have settled softly on my broken heart, and it, with the months past, has given the weary ravages of summer and fall a wonderful winter newness.

Tidings of comfort and joy are an actual reality, but they're not being brought by a man in a red suit or a baby in some straw, and most certainly not from a wife in a tight new dress. No, comfort and joy have finally appeared to me in the only way they ever could: from me.

I spent Thanksgiving taking out garbage at a soup kitchen. My family went to Sharon, to the house from which this tale originated. I chose to be by myself, and my guest list was complete. It's not possible, I now realize, to find peace in any other form but yourself. I looked for it in girlfriends; I looked for it in marriage. My children are the root of life and love, but if I can't be happy alone, then I can't be truly happy with them. Certainly, one cannot find true peace of mind and heart in someone else.

How many clichés would I have to go through to make the point that this has been the truth of things since the written word? Like the hero in this story, a little man who stands guard in front of a house that I now believe I was meant to find, he stands alone and has been trying to tell me every time I pull up: "Stand alone, stand alone, stand alone!" STAND.

He stands, without a reverse-racist lawn jockey wife, holding his lamp, and, in his molded concrete form, is what he is. I have been pulling up to this house that has been waiting for me (like the Overlook Hotel was waiting for Jack Torrance to fulfill his destiny, albeit a bit scarier), and acknowledging this strange little icon, this bizarre-looking messenger, and, in fact, hearing his message, but not feeling it.

I was brought to him, to Chickahominy, to find me. And I realize that since coming out of the stasis I was in for well over a decade, I buried myself under the covers, literally and figuratively. Perhaps all that sleep helped to physically preserve me, which is good because I will now need all the energy I can get to live the way I plan to live from now on. Yes, seeing other women has helped. So they were right.

"Get a girlfriend". I'll do you one better; "Get several."

But more than that, I now look at women as fascinating, desirable beings to spend time with, not some holder of secret happiness in a magic container inside their hearts that I can tap. They are they, and I am I.

There will no longer be a "we" for me.

I have my family, and we have come to an arrangement whereby I stay in the Old Greenwich house half the time, and my wife stays at View Street half the time. And then we switch. It works. On my days, I now get up at 6:30 in the morning, fix breakfast, pack backpacks, go over homework, make lunches, and write love notes to them in their snack bags. I dot the i in my daughter's name with a heart on her brown bag with a magic marker, and we dance to Maroon 5. Then, I walk them to school.

I pick them up after school, fix them dinner, do their homework, give them baths, practice piano, and teach them to help me KEEP THIS FUCKING HOUSE CLEAN. We dance to Coldplay, and then I read them stories, tuck them in, and kiss them. I am there in the next bedroom the whole blessed night.

Yes, it's that good.

I have my time with them, and then I look forward to my trek back to the other side of the tracks to pursue the other half of my life: the journey of self.

What my wife does, I do not know. I know she is happy, and I am so happy for her. I know of no one else who better deserves it. I will always love her, and we will always be together, bonded inexorably in the ties of our beloved children, but I no longer need to have her "back."

Such is the gift of Christmas this year.

Santa brought me something I always wanted; his sack was stuffed with me. That didn't sound right. Nonetheless.

As the wind rose and the cold of December came in like an old, unwanted but expected visitor, oddly, my arms and legs thawed. No wonder the M.R.I. didn't see the problem; it isn't designed to diagnose a broken heart. That's all it was.

And it didn't need a machine to fix it – the heart is like a lobster claw; it grows back.

We are alone. I have never been so alone as when I was married, but married or not, we can be happy as such, filling our lives with love, but not letting it consume us, control us, but most importantly for me, define us.

And so I get in my car. And then I come to this ramp.

This is the ramp they use to back boats into the harbor: the Byram

213

River boat ramp. It declines at an angle to allow boats to transition from their awkward cradles in dry dock to where they belong – the sea.

A boat engine will seize, sucking air because it needs water. So it's a transition ramp, a crossing, a bridge to home. The Byram Harbor ramp is where I took all my girls in my youth. I would park my 1969 red Volkswagen Beetle, with the crank-handle sunroof, down the ramp so the lapping surf would touch its front wheels. I would gauge, to the minute, when I needed to back up to avoid slipping on the slime and algae clinging to the concrete ramp into the harbor water. Once, I misjudged, and my girlfriend and I waved feverishly to a passing pickup truck to tow us out of the water because, after all, it would float, famous as it was to do so, but sink soon thereafter, for sure.

So I know this ramp. I stand here now on it, clutching both our rings.

I took a woman to this ramp on New Year's Eve and asked her to marry me. She said yes.

The ramp was snow-covered, and I had to gauge carefully how much time would pass before I had to put her Pontiac Grand Am into reverse to avoid hailing a stranger's kindness. We beat the shifting tides but were swallowed by the rolling bullshit of time.

Rolling like surf, it softened us, like beach glass – smooth edges, tossed away in a dance of tides and time. The waves erode things and make new things.

And something new is made now.

# —The End—

Made in the USA
Columbia, SC
23 February 2025

4e2d94fc-2109-48ab-a9bb-c258948f7ef4R02